MILITARY AND VETERAN ISSUES

ADAPTIVE SPORTS AND PARALYMPIC GRANT PROGRAMS FOR VETERANS

OVERVIEW, BREAKDOWNS AND ASSESSMENTS

MILITARY AND VETERAN ISSUES

Additional books in this series can be found on Nova's website under the Series tab.

Additional e-books in this series can be found on Nova's website under the eBooks tab.

MILITARY AND VETERAN ISSUES

ADAPTIVE SPORTS AND PARALYMPIC GRANT PROGRAMS FOR VETERANS

OVERVIEW, BREAKDOWNS AND ASSESSMENTS

DEVIN MORALES
EDITOR

New York

NOTICE TO THE READER

Library of Congress Cataloging-in-Publication Data

ISBN: 978-1-63484-916-6

Published by Nova Science Publishers, Inc. † New York

CONTENTS

PREFACE

VA's adaptive sports grant program distributes $8 million annually to organizations that provide sports activities for veterans and service members with disabilities. The U.S. Olympic Committee (USOC) played an intermediary role from fiscal year 2010, when the program was implemented, through 2013. USOC received funds from VA and subgranted them to selected grantees. VA is now responsible for selecting grantees and program administration. This book reviews how VA selected grantees to provide activities for veterans and service members with disabilities; how VA monitors grantees' use of funds; and what programs and activities were supported with fiscal year 2014 funds, and what is known about its benefits.

In: Adaptive Sports …
Editor: Devin Morales

ISBN: 978-1-63484-916-6

Chapter 1

ADAPTIVE SPORTS GRANT PROGRAM: VA HAS TAKEN STEPS TOWARD BETTER GRANTEE SELECTION AND OVERSIGHT, BUT ADDITIONAL ACTIONS NEEDED*

United States Government Accountability Office

ABBREVIATIONS

GAO	U.S. Government Accountability Office
OMB	Office of Management and Budget
USOC	U.S. Olympic Committee
VA	Department of Veterans Affairs

WHY GAO DID THIS STUDY

VA's adaptive sports grant program distributes $8 million annually to organizations that provide sports activities for veterans and service members

* This is an edited, reformatted and augmented version of a Congressional Research Service publication GAO-15-791, prepared for Members and Committees of Congress, dated September 2015.

with disabilities. The U.S. Olympic Committee (USOC) played an intermediary role from fiscal year 2010, when the program was implemented, through 2013. USOC received funds from VA and subgranted them to selected grantees. VA is now responsible for selecting grantees and program administration. Congress included a provision in statute for GAO to review VA's program management.

GAO reviewed (1) how VA selected grantees to provide activities for veterans and service members with disabilities; (2) how VA monitors grantees' use of funds; and (3) what programs and activities were supported with fiscal year 2014 funds, and what is known about its benefits. GAO reviewed a nongeneralizable sample of 16 of the 69 grant files accounting for about $3.7 million of the $8 million awarded in fiscal year 2014; and interviewed VA officials, as well as grantee officials and adaptive sports participants during site visits to adaptive sports events in three states, selected in part to ensure regional diversity.

What GAO Recommends

GAO recommends that VA (1) specify the number and frequency of annual site visits and remote audits, and (2) systematically identify and disseminate techniques for reducing no-shows. VA concurred with both recommendations.

What GAO Found

From December 2013 through September 2014, VA developed implementing regulations, announced availability of funding, and selected grantees—ultimately awarding 69 grants from a pool of 161 applications to receive funding under its adaptive sports grant program. VA selected grantees in three steps, including (1) eliminating non-qualifying applications, (2) scoring and ranking qualifying applications using nine criteria, such as strength of the proposed program concept, and (3) a final step that included, among other things, eliminating unnecessary costs from proposed budgets. VA officials said limited available time necessitated the use of a standard federal grant application form rather than one tailored for the program. Because the form did not include some information needed to assess applications—such as the roles of partner organizations—VA asked for narrative attachments. These attachments varied greatly in length and detail which VA officials said made their review quite labor intensive. In addition, some applications did not contain needed information. For example, 3 of the 16 grant files reviewed by GAO did not contain documentation of the grantee's financial management capabilities. VA customized its application form for fiscal year 2015, and VA officials said this led to a substantial improvement in the application process.

VA developed a grant monitoring approach for fiscal year 2014 grants that relied on quarterly and annual reports from grantees (containing information on financial and sports activities), site visits, and remote auditing of selected grantees. In the sample of 16 grant files reviewed, GAO found grantees generally complied with VA's quarterly reporting requirements. VA has improved the quarterly report template so that it requests information on time spent on direct personal interaction with participants. Through June 2015, VA provided GAO with reports of 8 visits covering 9 of its 69 grants. However, VA did not initiate a remote audit until August 2015. The agency developed a draft grant monitoring plan in the fourth quarter of fiscal year 2015, but the plan does not specify the number or frequency of site visits and remote audits. This omission risks the possibility that none will be performed in some years, or performed very late in the year, thus missing an opportunity for prompt detection of the misuse of funds.

The grants supported a variety of sports activities and afforded participant benefits such as socialization and improved personal independence, according to the participants, coaches, and grantee officials GAO interviewed. The 69 grantees in fiscal year 2014 planned activities that encompassed many different adaptive sports, with cycling, boating, and snow skiing among the most common. Overall, the allotment for administrative costs in grantees' budgets was about 5.7 percent of the total $8 million awarded in fiscal year 2014—below the statutory maximum of 7.5 percent. However, some grantee officials expressed concern about a significant no-show rate. VA officials confirmed that no-shows are a problem, and stated that they had shared information with some grantees about ways to reduce no-shows. However, they have not systematically gathered and disseminated such techniques to all grantees, which could promote higher attendance rates and maximum benefit of federal dollars.

September 28, 2015

The Honorable Johnny Isakson
Chairman
The Honorable Richard Blumenthal
Ranking Member
Committee on Veterans' Affairs
United States Senate

The Honorable Jeff Miller
Chairman

The Honorable Corrine Brown
Ranking Member
Committee on Veterans' Affairs
House of Representatives

In 2013, an estimated 3.6 million veterans had a disability due to service-related injuries and illnesses.[1] Due to advances in battlefield medicine a larger proportion of military personnel are surviving their injuries, though often with serious medical challenges including amputations, traumatic brain injuries, and post-traumatic stress disorder. In part to promote the lifelong health of veterans and service members with disabilities through regular participation in physical activity and sports, federal law authorized an adaptive sports grant program in 2008.[2] As reauthorized in 2013, the law tasks the Department of Veterans Affairs (VA) with making grants to eligible entities for planning, developing, managing, and implementing programs to provide adaptive sports opportunities for veterans and members of the armed services with disabilities. Initially authorized through fiscal year 2013, the program was reauthorized and amended in December 2013, with the reauthorization stating that VA can provide funding for adaptive sports opportunities occurring though fiscal year 2016.[3] The reauthorization also included a provision that GAO submit a report on the use of grants under the program.[4]

Our objectives in this review were to determine (1) how the VA adaptive sports grant program selected grantees to provide adaptive sports activities for veterans and service members with disabilities; (2) how the program monitors grantees' use of grant funds; and (3) what programs and activities have been supported with fiscal year 2014 grant funds, and what is known about how veterans and service members with disabilities may have benefited from these programs and activities.[5]

To address the objectives outlined above, we limited our review to program grants made using fiscal year 2014 funds, which supported grantee activities that were to take place in fiscal year 2015. Because our audit work began and ended during VA's first year of monitoring grantees, our work on VA's grantee monitoring generally covered the first two quarters of fiscal year 2015—October 2014 through March 2015. We reviewed relevant federal laws and regulations, government-wide and VA grants management policies and other grants management criteria, VA's July 2014 Notice of Funding Availability, quarterly status reports submitted by selected grantees for the first half of fiscal year 2015, and VA site visit reports of the grantees completed through June 2015. We also obtained VA data on grantee budgets and proposed activities. We interviewed VA officials about this data and determined that it was sufficiently reliable for the purposes of this report. We also reviewed relevant grants management criteria, such as VA's agency-wide grants management policies. Further, we obtained VA data on grantee budgets and proposed activities. To better understand VA's approach to grantee selection and oversight, we also reviewed a sample of VA's grant files— 16 of the 69 grants awarded in fiscal year 2014. We selected these grants to include all 10 grants of $250,000 or more, and 6 grants that were randomly selected in a manner to ensure that we obtained at least one grantee from each category of grantees—national, regional, and community-based organizations. In addition, we ensured that selected grantees included representation of different geographic regions. While this sample is not generalizable to all 69 grants, it accounts for about $3.7 million, or 46 percent, of the $8 million in the grant funds awarded in fiscal year 2014. We also conducted interviews with officials of VA and the U.S. Olympic Committee (USOC), the latter of which had previously been responsible for administering the program. Finally, we conducted site visits to three events sponsored by selected grantees in Indiana, Illinois, and North Carolina. We selected events that occurred during our review while also considering regional diversity and travel considerations. During the visits, we observed sports events, and interviewed sponsoring organization officials, participant athletes, coaches, and instructors. In addition, we reviewed relevant documents and interviewed VA officials regarding changes to the grant application and review process in fiscal year 2015.

We conducted this performance audit from November 2014 through September 2015 in accordance with generally accepted government auditing standards. Those standards require that we plan and perform the audit to obtain sufficient, appropriate evidence to provide a reasonable basis for our findings and conclusions based on our audit objectives. We believe that the evidence we obtained provides a reasonable basis for our findings and conclusions based on our audit objectives.

BACKGROUND

Participation in adaptive sports—sports that have been specifically adapted or created for persons with disabilities—has been recognized by experts as an important means of rehabilitation for people with physical and other disabilities, including veterans and members of the armed services.

In 2008, federal law authorized VA to establish a grant program to fund adaptive sports for veterans and members of the armed services with disabilities. First operated using fiscal year 2010 funds, the program is authorized to support activities that will facilitate, encourage, and sustain participation in adaptive sports activities. Under the program, grants are made to qualifying organizations, referred to in the law as eligible entities, that will plan, develop, manage and implement programs to provide adaptive sports opportunities. To be eligible for a grant, an organization must be a non-federal entity with significant experience in managing a large-scale adaptive sports program. Such experience must be with programs that are either (1) affiliated with a National Paralympic Committee or a National Governing Body authorized to provide Paralympic sports, (2) an adaptive sports program of a National Governing Body that meets certain other requirements, or (3) an adaptive sports program in which at least 50 persons with disabilities participate or in which the participants with disabilities reside in at least five different congressional districts.[6] Since fiscal year 2010, VA has allocated $8 million per year for the program.

During the program's first four fiscal years—2010 through 2013—the USOC served an intermediary role in program management, receiving grant funds from VA and sub-granting them to organizations that provided adaptive sports opportunities and events.[7] In 2012, we reported on the program's actual or planned activities in fiscal years 2010 to 2012, when USOC was involved.[8] At that time, we found several shortcomings in program reporting and oversight practices. For example, we found that expenditure reporting practices for grantees were not consistent with federal internal control standards, and that VA was not performing on-site or remote monitoring to verify how funds were being used. In addition, we reported that in fiscal year 2011 \$3.1 million of the \$7.5 million annually provided by VA—about 40 percent—was absorbed by USOC for its operations, personnel, and administrative costs. We made several recommendations aimed at improving grantee reporting and encouraged VA to review implementation of USOC's monitoring plan. VA's implementation of the program substantially addresses these recommendations.[9] As appropriate, we refer to these recommendations and related VA actions to address them later in this report.

In December 2013, the program was reauthorized with a number of changes. The reauthorization eliminated USOC's role and instead provides that VA can award grants to eligible entities. In addition, the law placed specific limits on grantees' use of grant funds for administrative and personnel costs. For grants supporting adaptive sports opportunities taking place during fiscal year 2015, grantees can allocate no more than 7.5 percent to such costs; in fiscal year 2016 and thereafter, grantees will be limited to 5 percent. Law and regulation include other requirements for VA and grantees. For example, the adaptive sports program's authorizing statute and regulations outline a number of criteria that guide grant application review and selection, including requirements that applicants clearly state the sports activities to be provided, clearly define program objectives, and describe the adequacy of their program management structure.[10] In addition, applications must include detailed descriptions of any partnerships and the grant funds that will be provided to any partners; the anticipated personnel, travel, and administrative costs paid for with grant funding; and the performance metrics to be used to evaluate the effectiveness of the activities carried out with grant funds. VA grant programs are also subject to government-wide grants management requirements.[11]

In its first two years of awarding grants, VA has awarded grants near the end of the fiscal year for use by grantees to support activities to be carried out in the following fiscal year. For example, organizations that were awarded grants in fiscal year 2014 have used fiscal year 2014 funds to support adaptive sports activities during fiscal year 2015. Similarly, grantees will use grants awarded in fiscal year 2015 to support adaptive sports activities that will occur primarily during fiscal year 2016. Except where specifically noted, this report refers only to activities and events pertaining to grants awarded in fiscal year 2014.

GRANT SELECTION PROCESS HAD LIMITATIONS IN FISCAL YEAR 2014, BUT VA IMPLEMENTED AN IMPROVED PROCESS IN FISCAL YEAR 2015

VA Faced a Tight Timeframe in Selecting Fiscal Year 2014 Grantees

In fiscal year 2014, the first year VA was responsible for selecting eligible entities to receive grants under the adaptive sports grant program, VA officials reported challenges because of tight time frames to obtain and review grant applications and the lack of a standard application form tailored for the adaptive sports grant program. (See fig. 1 for a timeline of events.)

As figure 1 illustrates, days after publishing the program's interim final rule on July 1, 2014[12], VA issued a Notice of Funding Availability that informed potential applicants of the availability of grant funds for adaptive sports activities.[13] The notice also specified the procedures for submitting an application, and outlined the selection criteria VA would use to select grants for funding. VA received 161 applications by the August 11, 2014 application deadline, and then reviewed and evaluated the applications in several stages. In the first stage, VA staff rejected 68 applications that they determined did not meet the minimum eligibility requirements. According to VA officials and our review of available documentation, these applications were rejected for a variety of reasons, including ineligibility of the applicant for a grant, an incomplete application, or the ineligibility of the activities proposed for funding. In the second stage, the remaining 93 applications were scored and ranked by a three-person review panel consisting of VA adaptive sports experts who evaluated the applications according to nine criteria outlined in the Notice of Funding Availability (see sidebar).[14] Based on the total of the three panelists' scores, each application was ranked against the others, resulting in 81 applications that met or exceeded a designated cutoff score. However, because these applicants' proposed budgets collectively exceeded the $8 million allocated for the program in fiscal year 2014, a third and final stage was necessary to eliminate additional applications.[15] According to VA staff, the additional evaluation emphasized applications that combined low risk and high potential return. For example, it sought to ensure that proposed activities were occurring in areas with a large population of veterans with disabilities.

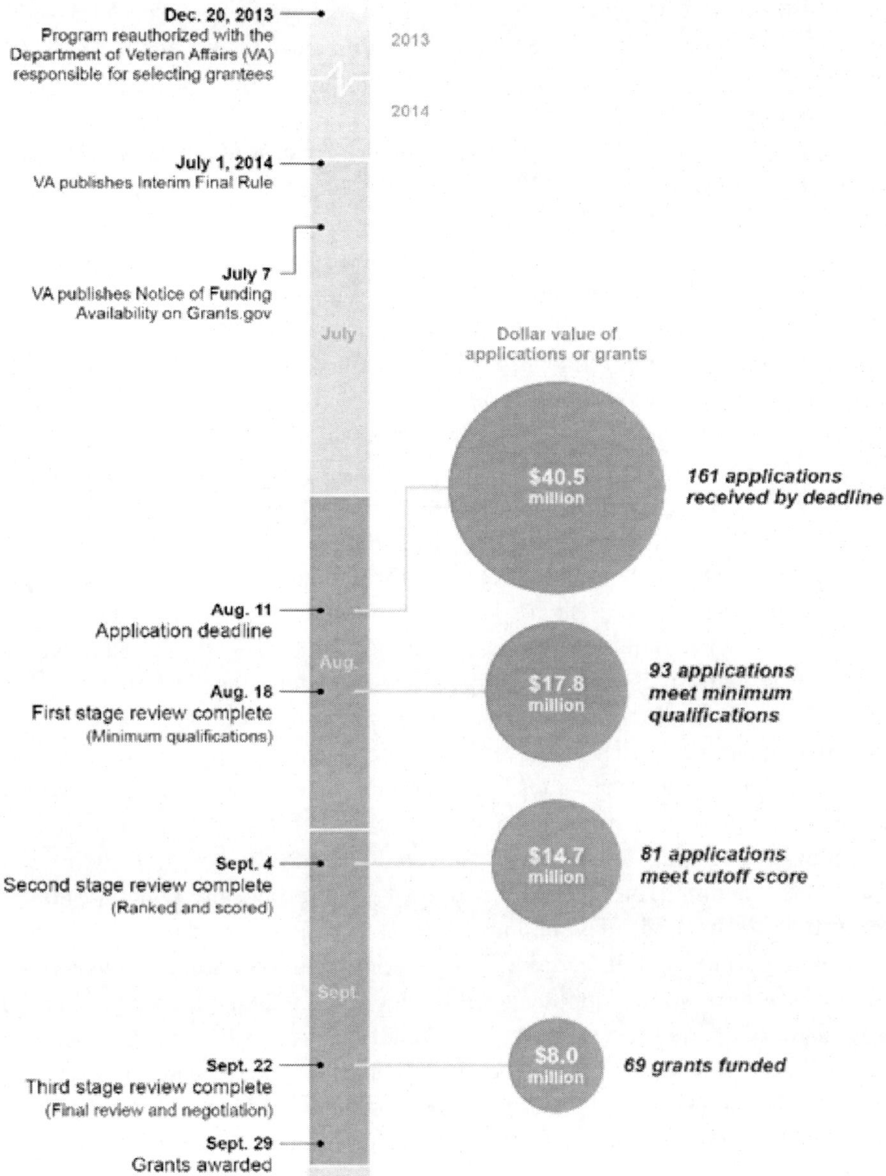

Source: GAO presentation of VA data. | GAO-15-791.

Figure 1. Key Events and Results of Fiscal Year 2014 Application and Review Process for Veterans Affairs' Adaptive Sports Grant Program.

In some cases, some aspects of a proposal were accepted and others rejected to make the proposed grant amount smaller. At the end of this process, VA selected 69 applications to which the $8 million allocated for the program in fiscal year 2014 was awarded.

VA officials told us that completing all tasks necessary to award the grants before the end of fiscal year 2014 was very challenging—in part because of the limited time frame and because managing the solicitation and selection of grant applicants was a new experience for the responsible VA unit. However, VA officials explained that the alternative would have been that no program activities would have been funded with fiscal year 2014 dollars.[16] Officials told us that developing and publishing the interim final rule to govern the program within about 6 months required considerable effort. VA officials also told us that development and authorization of an application form tailored to the program was not possible within the deadlines they faced in fiscal year 2014. Instead they opted to use a standard federal grant applications form—SF-424— developed by OMB.[17] Because law and regulation required the program's grant applications to include information that the SF-424 forms are not designed to include—such as a description of the roles of any partner organization—VA required narrative attachments to this standard application form. These narratives varied greatly in length, detail, and format. According to one VA official, they ranged from about 7 pages to about 60 pages.

As a result, according to VA officials, the review and approval process for fiscal year 2014 was very labor-intensive, and VA officials said staff had to engage in extensive communications and negotiations with applicants. For example, VA officials told us they conducted extensive negotiations with some applicants regarding the cost and scope of their proposals, with the aim of controlling costs and maximizing the benefits that program funds would provide to participants. In addition, VA officials said that, despite repeated VA communication, some applicants did not understand the limitation on administrative expenses. Under this limitation, for activities taking place during fiscal year 2015, grantees could allocate no more than 7.5 percent of the grant amount to administrative expenses, including any costs associated with employees other than those who directly provided coaching and training for participants.[18] This misunderstanding may have been unintentionally reinforced by the budget categories used in the standard federal application form, which do not distinguish between these two types of personnel costs. For example, the standard form includes a line for personnel expenses, but does not distinguish between costs attributable to coaching and instruction, and other types of personnel costs.

Documentation of Important Aspects of Grantee Applications Was Missing or Limited

Federal law, VA regulation, and grant management principles dictate that a number of requirements be followed during the application and selection process. For example, the program statute and VA regulations require that an applicant submit a detailed description of its financial controls, including methods to track expenditure of grant funds, that a grantee observe the applicable percent limit on administrative expenses, and that any partnerships be described, including the amount of funds that will be made available to each partner. Despite VA's efforts to ensure completeness of grant applications, our review of 16 fiscal year 2014 grant files and other VA documentation found that in some cases aspects of grant applications were not well documented. For example, VA developed a standard checklist—the VA Administrative and Financial Review Questionnaire for Grantees— for applicants to attest to various aspects of their administrative and financial policies and procedures. While this checklist was not required, VA officials told us that they treated the satisfactory completion of this form as sufficient evidence that the grantee could adequately safeguard and account for grant funds.[19]

However, 3 of 16 grant files we reviewed contained neither this form nor any other documentation of the administrative and financial capabilities of the grantee. The forms of 3 others indicated that these grantees lacked certain administrative and financial policies and procedures. For example, one grantee indicated on its form that it did not have a written accounting manual or written policies and procedures for managing finances.

Other aspects of some grantee applications were also limited. For example, 7 of the 16 grant applications we reviewed lacked clear documentation that the 7.5 percent limit on administrative expenses had been observed in proposed budgets.[20] Similarly, we found that in 3 cases, full documentation of intended grantee partnerships was not clear. For example, one grantee's application narrative referred to partners but did not specify the role of the partner organizations. As discussed in the next subsection, VA subsequently took action to keep instances of such documentation issues from recurring in future grant application and award processes.

VA's New Application Form and Other Changes Address Earlier Limitations

The fiscal year 2015 application process differed in significant ways from the fiscal year 2014 process.[21] Importantly, VA developed a new application form tailored to the adaptive sports grant program.[22] As summarized in table 1, our review indicates that this new form addresses the review difficulties and documentation limitations the program experienced in fiscal year 2014. For example, whereas the fiscal year 2014 application form did not require applicants to distinguish between the two types of personnel costs so as to meet the limit on total administrative costs, the new form does. Similarly, the new form requires that applicants explicitly identify partner organizations, including their locations and roles.

Table 1. Differences between FY 2014 and 2015 Grant Application Formats for Veterans Affairs' Adaptive Sports Grant Program

Component	FY 2014	FY 2015	Potential improvement
Length of narrative attachments	No limit	3-page limit	Facilitate VA review and identification of key descriptive elements
Identification of services	No specific format	Planned events and services must be listed on a single page, including projected start/end dates	Facilitate VA identification of specific, quantifiable services
Limit on Administrative Costs	No distinction between the two types of personnel costs	Separate budget lines for personnel costs attributable to coaching and training, and administrative personnel costs	Better ensure that administrative costs as defined for this program will be below statutory limit of 5 percent for adaptive sports opportunities taking place in fiscal year 2016 and later
Partnering and Collaborating	Not included	Partner organizations, their locations, and what they will do must be listed	Clarify identities and planned activities of partner organizations

Component	FY 2014	FY 2015	Potential improvement
Equipment	Included as budget line item	Requires a listing of all equipment, including type, make/model, and value	Help reduce confusion over goods categorized as “supplies” versus “equipment”
Outreach	Not included	Specific section for description of outreach efforts	Better description of grantee efforts to publicize activities funded by grant.

Source: GAO analysis of VA documents and application forms. I GAO-15-791.

In addition to the new form, other aspects of the fiscal year 2015 application process increased the likelihood that VA would receive more complete application packages and conduct a more efficient review. While applicants had 5 weeks to prepare and submit grant applications after publication of the Notice of Funding Availability in fiscal year 2014, in fiscal year 2015 they had 9 weeks. In fiscal year 2015 VA also required applicants to submit the Administrative and Financial Review Questionnaire, which was optional in fiscal year 2014 and which inquires about an applicant’s administrative and financial policies, procedures, accounting, and management of grants.

Because VA was reviewing fiscal year 2015 grant applications at the time we were completing our audit work, we did not review the applications or accompanying documentation and cannot independently assess their quality compared to those submitted in fiscal year 2014. However, VA officials told us in July 2015 that the new application resulted in a much improved and more efficient application and review process. Specifically, the application form instructs applicants to provide required information or leave a visible blank, and so VA officials noted that the fiscal year 2015 applications have been more consistently complete and the rate of rejection of incomplete applications much lower. Also, they said VA’s review has been much less laborious in fiscal year 2015. Finally, according to VA, the new form facilitated a more comprehensive approach to comparing proposed budgets among the grant applications.

VA MONITORS GRANTEES IN SEVERAL WAYS, BUT ITS APPROACH FOR 2014 GRANTEES HAD LIMITATIONS

The Design of VA's Monitoring Approach is Consistent with Grants Management Criteria, but Further Improvements Could be Made

VA's approach to monitoring grantees, as outlined in VA grants management policy and an agency memorandum on monitoring techniques, includes regular grantee reporting, supplemented with monitoring through detailed site visits and desk audits of selected grantees. This approach is consistent with the Uniform Guidance,[23] and is intended to help ensure that grantees are providing adaptive sports opportunities to veterans and service members, according to the terms of their grant agreements with VA. It is also intended to help ensure that VA grant funds are being managed according to federal requirements, as reflected in the grant agreements. In addition, grantee monitoring can provide VA with useful information to measure the grant program's performance and for reporting to the Congress and the public.

VA requires that all grantees submit quarterly and annual reports.[24] VA reviews these reports to ensure that grantees are operating according to the terms of their grant agreements.[25] While only annual reports are required under the program's statute, VA requires grantees to report on performance quarterly because, according to VA officials, this helps to provide for more frequent monitoring of grantees.[26]

To ensure that grantees' quarterly reports include consistent information in accordance with statutory and regulatory requirements, VA created a standard quarterly report template, adapted from a USOC template. As summarized in table 2, VA's quarterly report template contains data required from grantees under VA's program regulations.[27] For each grant, VA customized the template to show the activities the grantee agreed to provide; and a budget showing the amount awarded, broken out into several categories. According to VA officials, they identified the activities and budget amounts by reviewing each grantee's application. Grantees are expected to submit an updated report each quarter to VA. The quarterly report format is consistent with GAO's 2012 recommendations, in that it (1) requires reporting of the expenditure of VA grant program funds, excluding funds from other sources; and (2) is formatted to provide consistent and non-duplicative reporting of activities and numbers of participants.[28] Table 2 summarizes how VA translated the information required of grantees into the quarterly report format.

Table 2. Comparison of Quarterly Report Requirements to VA's Quarterly Report Format

Information required by VA program regulation	*Corresponding section of quarterly report*
Detailed record of individual adaptive sports activities conducted	*Deliverables Progress*: VA provides the list of activities the grantee must complete under VA's grant. The grantee is to provide information on its progress in completing each activity. *Activities/Events:* The grantee is to report the number of events it held, by category (practice/training events, camps, clinics and competitions).
Record of activities carried out through partnerships	*Partnerships:* The grantee is to identify organizations with which it has partnered, such as VA medical facilities, military installations, and non-profit organizations; and describe how it collaborated with each organization.
Number of veterans and service members served	*Deliverables Progress:*The grantee is to provide a count of the number of veterans and service members participating in its activities. *Unique Veterans:* The grantee is to identify each participant, by name and ZIP Code.
Detailed accounting of how funds were used	*Budget:* VA provides the amount of funding available to the grantee, broken down by expenditure categories such as Travel and Personnel. The grantee is to provide amounts spent to date, and amounts remaining. Personnel costs are to be reported so that a clear distinction is made between costs attributable to direct coaching and training of participants, versus other types of personnel costs. *Equipment:* If the grantee's deliverables and budget include equipment purchases, the grantee is to provide a description of each piece of equipment.
Locations of activities	VA's template used in fiscal year 2015 did not specifically include a place for this information. However, in some cases, VA included locations of some events in the Deliverables Progress section of the template.

Table 2. (Continued)

Information required by VA program regulation	*Corresponding section of quarterly report*
Detailed record of personnel time spent providing adaptive sports activities 1) through direct interaction with participants, and 2) activities not involving direct personal interactions	VA's report template used in fiscal year 2015 did not include a place for this information.

Source: GAO analysis based on VA's adaptive sports grant regulations pertaining to reporting requirements (38 C.F.R. § 77.16(a) and (b)) and its Adaptive Sports Grants quarterly reporting template. | GAO-15-791

Note: In addition to the required information listed in this table, VA provides space in the quarterly report for the grantee to describe how it conducted outreach to veterans and service members; the impact of its VA-funded activities on veterans and service members; and challenges it faces in completing the required activities under the VA grant.

As indicated in table 2, VA's quarterly report template did not require grantees to provide all of the information required by program regulations. For example, VA program regulations require grantees to include in their reports detailed records of the time involved in providing adaptive sports activities through direct personal interaction with adaptive sports participants, such as coaching or instruction, versus time spent on other adaptive sports activities.[29] However, during fiscal year 2015, VA did not require grantees to add this information to the quarterly reports.[30] We pointed out this omission to VA staff, and in August 2015, they provided a draft revised quarterly report format, where grantees are to provide information on time spent providing direct instruction to participants. A VA official indicated that they intended to further revise the template so that it also required grantees to report staff time spent on matters other than direct personal interaction with participants, as required by regulations. They expected to complete the template revision before the start of fiscal year 2016.

VA's program regulations also require grantees to identify the locations of their adaptive sports activities. However, VA did not provide a specific place for grantees to report the locations of their activities.[31] VA has revised its quarterly report format to have grantees identify locations of their activities. Improved information from grantees could help VA assess the extent of geographic coverage of adaptive sports opportunities.

In addition to quarterly reporting by all grantees, VA's grantee monitoring approach calls for monitoring of selected grantees through conducting site visits and desk audits, although the reporting format for the latter has not been established. A site visit involves a visit to a grantee's offices to review financial and other records, a visit to a grantee's adaptive sports event, or both. The reviewing official is to assess the extent to which the grantee is providing activities according to the grant agreement. Also, the reviewer is to assess the soundness of the grantee's financial management of VA grant funds, as well as the grantee's financial controls. To record the results of the assessments for use by VA program officials, the reviewer prepares a site visit report using a standard VA format. A desk audit (also known as a remote audit), according to VA officials, involves asking the grantee to provide documentation to support an assessment of grantee financial management issues that might be of concern. VA may, for example, ask to see receipts for equipment or transportation ticket purchases or ask for documentation of how the calculation of staff days spent on providing services is made. A VA official stated that desk audits will likely be tailored to the circumstances as appropriate.

For both site visits and desk audits, VA employs a selective monitoring approach—based on risk—to help focus its limited resources on grantees at highest risk of failing to perform or mismanaging funds. Such an approach is consistent with our prior work, which found that risk-based monitoring can help agencies identify grantees that need additional attention; for example, using limited resources to visit higher-risk grantees.[32]

According to VA officials, one criterion for assessing risk is the awarded amount. Officials said that they tend to select grantees receiving less funding for desk audits, and grantees receiving more funding for site visits, because those receiving larger grants are at risk of losing more dollars in case of financial mismanagement. VA also said that they use information from application reviews, such as assessments of financial controls, and grantees' previous experience providing adaptive sports programs, in deciding whether a desk audit or site visit is warranted. Another consideration is the scope of a grantee's event. A VA official said that a site visit may be scheduled to a multi-sport event, such as one of the regional Valor Games, where a grantee may be collaborating with other adaptive sports providers, including other VA grantees.[33] To economize on monitoring costs, VA uses geographic considerations as well. For example, VA officials said that a site visit may be planned if it would cover several grantees headquartered in the same area.

Although VA officials provided us their policy on monitoring of grant funded activities, for most of fiscal year 2015 they did not have a written monitoring plan. Best practices in grants management suggest that risk-based monitoring helps agencies ensure adequate grantee financial management and performance.[34] Also, planning is part of an agency's internal control system, which helps program managers achieve desired results through effective stewardship of public resources, such as grant funds.[35] For example, by documenting and using written criteria for determining which grantees need closer monitoring, VA could be better positioned to help prevent mismanagement of funds and poor program performance. We discussed this issue with VA staff earlier in our review, and in August 2015, they provided us with their draft monitoring plan. According to a VA official, VA expects to complete this plan early in fiscal year 2016. VA's draft plan describes a monitoring approach consistent with VA grants management policy. However, the draft plan lacks certain elements, such as information on the number and frequency of site visits and desk audits. Promising practices in ensuring adequate grantee financial systems and proper use of grant funds include an agency reviewing a target number of grantees each year. For example, one agency requires reviews of 10 percent of all of its grantees each year as a mechanism to enhance grantee accountability.[36] A grantee monitoring plan that addresses the number and frequency of reviews throughout the year can help VA ensure that it is monitoring grantees on an ongoing basis, to prevent, and promptly detect, misuse of grant funds.[37]

The Implementation of VA's Monitoring Strategy Has Identified a Number of Issues

At the time of our review, VA was implementing two main methods of its monitoring approach—quarterly grantee reporting and VA site visits. Almost all of the grantees whose files we reviewed submitted their quarterly reports on time. For 13 of the 16 grants, the grantees submitted their first quarter fiscal year 2015 reports on time, and all submitted their second quarter reports on time. We found that, in general, the grantees provided the information VA requested. Also, in our review of the selected grantee files, we found evidence that VA reviewed the quarterly reports to ensure that grantees were operating according to the terms of their grant agreements with VA.

For 6 of the first-quarter and 12 of the second-quarter reports we reviewed, we found that VA identified issues for follow up, and requested additional information from grantees.[38] Table 3 describes examples of the types of issues VA identified in the quarterly reports we reviewed.

Table 3. Examples of Issues VA Identified in Reviews of Grantees' First and Second Quarter Fiscal Year 2015 Reports

Type of Issue	Specific issues and VA and grantee actions
Information missing or unnecessary information included	•VA noted that a grantee had partnerships with military facilities that were not listed in its first-quarter report. VA asked for additional information on partnerships. Grantee provided additional information in its second quarter report. •Grantee submitted a list of unique participants with some participants' home ZIP Codes missing. VA noted, in a message to grantees, that ZIP Codes are required to identify unique participants. Grantee provided additional ZIP Code information in second quarter report. •Grantee provided unnecessary personal information on unique participants. VA noted that it only requires names and home ZIP Codes. Grantee removed the unnecessary information from its report for the second quarter.
Budget discrepancy	•Two grantees incorrectly categorized expenditures for supplies as equipment purchases[a]; VA asked the grantees to correct the matter. One grantee corrected its second-quarter report to show no equipment purchases. A VA official stated that the other grantee is expected to correct the problem in its third quarter report. •VA requested a clarification of a grantee's reporting of administrative and personnel costs. VA discussed accounting for administrative costs with the grantee during a site visit. The grantee agreed to make corrections in its third quarter report.
Other issues	•VA asked grantee to confirm its ability to complete planned activities with available funding. The grantee responded that it was seeking additional funding from other sources.

Sources: Quarterly reports to VA by selected grantees; related documentation of VA communications with grantees; and discussions with VA officials. | GAO-15-791.

[a]Consistent with the definition of "equipment" for grants management purposes, VA only requested details of purchases of items costing $5,000 or more. See 2 C.F.R. § 200.33; 38 C.F.R. § 43.3.

We reviewed reports on the results of 8 VA site visits, covering 9 of its 69 grants, conducted from November 2014 through June 2015.39 Six of the 8 site visits occurred at grantees' adaptive sports events; the remaining 2 visits occurred at grantees' headquarters. As summarized in table 4, the reports identified several types of issues, although none of the issues reflected grantee noncompliance. In each of the 8 reports we reviewed, VA officials provided notes on how grantees operated their events and the financial management of VA grant funds. Several of the reports also made suggestions for improvements in these areas.

Table 4. Examples of Issues VA Identified During VA Site Visits to Grantees

Type of issue	Specific issues and VA suggestions for improvement
Event attendance	•One event was not well-attended, as there were only three participants. This was, in part, attributed to schedule conflicts between the event supported by the adaptive sports grant and other organizations' adaptive sports events. VA suggested that the grantee coordinate its events with other adaptive sports providers, such as military adaptive sports programs, to avoid future scheduling conflicts. •At one event with several activities, some veterans were not participating in all scheduled activities. Also, VA noted that the grantee collected insufficient information on which participants were veterans. VA suggested to grantee officials that for future events, the officials should improve their tracking of actual participation in its scheduled activities and collect information on veteran participants in its event registration system.
Potential change in grant terms	•During one event, the grantee asked VA if it could send instructors to a different training course than the one it identified in its application. VA noted that such a change in grant terms would require formal VA approval.

Source: GAO analysis of VA site visit reports, obtained from VA. | GAO-15-791.

Through July 2015, VA officials told us that the agency had not conducted any desk audits of fiscal year 2014 grantees. VA officials explained that at the start of fiscal year 2015, desk audits were intended to form a portion of the monitoring strategy, but they have been deferred due primarily to a large workload. In August 2015, a VA official stated that they had initiated a desk audit of one grantee.

VA GRANTS FUNDED A RANGE OF ADAPTIVE SPORTS ACTIVITIES, BUT SOME GRANTEES EXPRESSED CONCERN WITH NO-SHOWS

Fiscal Year 2014 Grants Funded Many Distinct Sport Activities

The 69 adaptive sports grants awarded by VA in fiscal year 2014 supported a wide range of activities, with cycling, boating, snow skiing, and archery among the most frequent (see fig. 2).

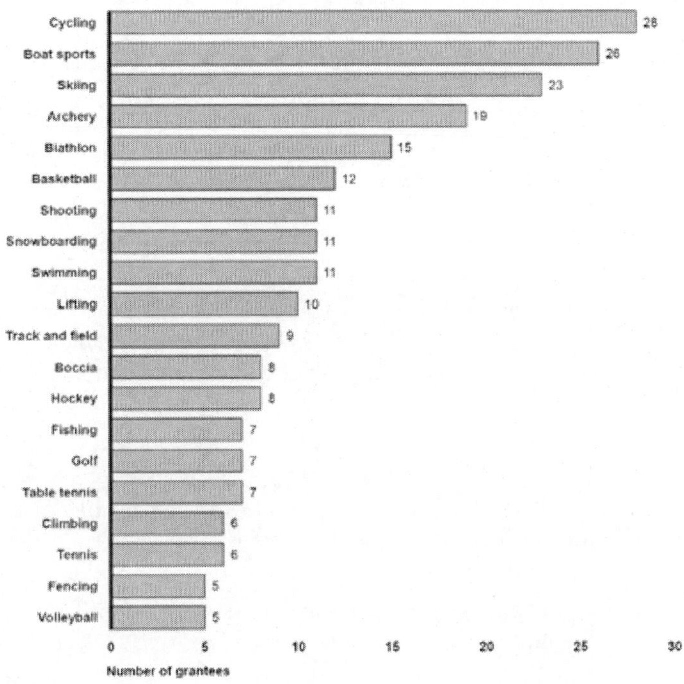

Source: GAO presentation of VA data. | GAO-15-791.

Note: This summary description of sports and activities represents the sports that fiscal year 2014 grantees planned to support at the outset of the grant period. However, because planned activities may have been modified during the implementation period, the end-of-year numbers may differ slightly from those presented. For example, in one of its quarterly reports, one grantee reported on a martial arts program that had not been envisioned at the time of the application. The boat sports category includes canoeing, rowing, and sailing and other similar activities.

Figure 2. Number of Adaptive Sports Grants Supporting Various Sports, FY 2014.

Some grants were focused on activities in a single location and/or sport, while others planned to support a variety of sports events. For example, one grant targeted recreational rowing for veterans with disabilities in five locations across the country, while another grant aimed to provide a variety of physical fitness activities in one state. Another grantee committed to provide more than seven different sports for paralyzed veterans in more than 30 locations across the country.

The activities supported by these 69 grants also targeted athletes with a range of disabilities (see table 5). A sport or an adaptation may be aimed at participants with a specific type of disability, or may be suitable for participants with a range of disabilities.

Table 5. Descriptions of How Selected Sports Can be Adapted for Persons with Disabilities

Disability	Adaptation by Sport
Blind/Vision Impaired	Tandem cycling: Vision-impaired athlete sits in second seat behind a sighted pilot, learning skills such as starting, turning, and stopping the bicycle. Goalball: Sport designed specifically for the vision-impaired in which teams alternately defend their goal and attack opponents' goal using a ball containing an audible bell.
Amputees	Sitting volleyball:Court size, height of net, and other aspects of traditional volleyball are modified to adapt to limited mobility of athletes. Archery: Archers with only one arm can steady the bow with one arm and use a mouth tab to pull and release the string.
Spinal Cord Injury/Paralysis	Handcycling: Riders use a specially-designed three-wheel cycle powered by hands and arms. Rider is either upright or recumbent. Adaptive skiing: Participant can sit in a molded seat attached to a single ski, using two "outrigger" skis controlled by the arms, for balance and steering.
Traumatic Brain Injury, Stroke, or Post-Traumatic Stress Disorder	Various sports: A variety of sports may be suitable, but specialized coaches and instructors may be needed.

Source: GAO presentation of descriptive information from various sources. | GAO-15-791.

To support these activities, grantees planned to spend grant funds in various budget categories. The largest categories for the 69 fiscal year 2014 grants were travel, including transportation, lodging, and subsistence for athletes, coaches, and other officials involved in meeting program objectives; operations, including such expenses as facility rentals and ski lift tickets; and supplies, including purchase of adaptive bicycles, watercraft, and bows and arrows (see fig. 3). Importantly, a total of about $459,000—about 5.7 percent of the total $8 million awarded— was budgeted as administrative costs. This included both normal administrative costs as well as personnel costs associated with grant activities but not attributable to time spent coaching or training participants. The amount was below the 7.5 percent statutory limit for activities carried out in fiscal year 2015.

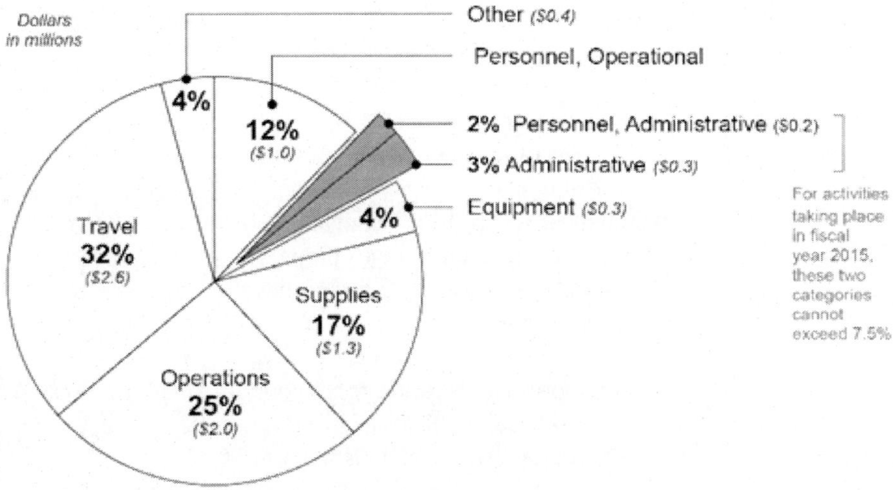

Source: GAO presentation of VA data. | GAO-15-791.

Note: Percentages do not equal 100 percent and dollar values do not equal $8.0 million due to rounding.

Figure 3. Total Proposed Spending, by Budget Category, by VA Adaptive Sports Grant Program Grantees, Fiscal Year 2014.

Participants and Others Report Enhanced Physical, Emotional, and Social Well-Being from Adaptive Sports Activities

Participants, grantee officials, and coaches we interviewed generally said that adaptive sports activities are beneficial to veterans and service members in multiple ways (see table 6.)[40] These benefits include improved family and social relationships, emotional health, levels of independence and life skills, and physical well-being. Several interviewees—including participants and grantee officials—said adaptive sports can have a transformative effect on a veteran with disabilities. One official said he sees disabled veterans who have been inactive for many years participate in adaptive sports, resulting in a significant life change. Another official said some veterans with disabilities get accustomed to being taken care of, which can amplify their disabilities. He recalled that at one sports clinic funded by the grant program, a blind veteran asked to be guided to another part of the sports facility and, after some good-natured ribbing by his teammates, was convinced he could navigate on his own.

Table 6. Statements about Benefits of Adaptive Sports Activities by VA Adaptive Sports Grant Coaches, Grantee Officials, and Participants

Benefit	Statement summaries
Social	Coach: One of the main benefits of the event—an annual event held in North Carolina that includes a variety of sports, including air rifle, sitting volleyball, table tennis and cycling— is that it encourages participants to be more social. The event helps to create a support network, and sometimes seeing others in various stages of recovery helps with recovery because they know they are not alone. Coach: Sports such as archery are good for veterans in that it gets them off their couches to spend time with their peers; some encourage other veterans to participate. Grantee official: Adaptive sporting events are a benefit for caregivers because they provide support for them as well.
Emotional	Participant: One participant said after he went blind, he also lost his career as a heavy equipment operator and became very depressed. Playing goalball changed this, he said. Coach: Some men, for example, Vietnam veterans, who had been convinced for years that they could not play any sports, have literally come out of a 40-year "funk" by playing goalball and making it a part of their lives. To say that the sport is fulfilling is an understatement; in some cases, the sport becomes participants' primary topic of conversation. Grantee official: Sports become an outlet for the intense, competitive nature that can typify pre-injury veterans.

Benefit	Statement summaries
Family Relationships	Participant: One participant, the father of two children, said the renewed confidence he found in sports has helped him develop a closer bond with his children. Grantee official: Inactivity lead to other problems such as marital strife; adaptive sports can be an important outlet.
Independence/Life Skills	Participant: Participation in adaptive sports led to the ability to navigate airports, something one athlete said he would not have attempted in the past. Participant: Archery has led to improved focus and concentration. Coach: Adaptive sports facilitated overall physical rehabilitation, said a coach, and helped skills as basic as being able to walk in a straight line.
Physical Well-Being	Participant: Participation in adaptive skiing and other sports renewed his interest in athletics and has had considerable health benefits—he lost 15 pounds and, as a diabetic, experienced a significant improvement in his blood sugar level. Coach: A sport like rowing is good for someone with a disability because it is a low-impact, full-body exercise with cardiovascular, muscular, and flexibility benefits. Grantee official: Archery can help someone with a new spinal cord injury, or someone who has not been physically active for a long time, develop core muscle strength. Coach: Veterans and service members gain physical and mental health advantages from activities like sitting volleyball.

Source: GAO discussions with athletes, coaches, and other stakeholders. | GAO-15-791.

Several experts we spoke with stressed the importance of sustained involvement in adaptive sports as the key to long-term benefits. According to one adaptive sports expert familiar with the grant program, the important thing is whether or not the event helps fuel a persistent participation in the sport and thereby contributes to a balanced and active life. One of the grantees we visited considered the opportunity that applicants would have to continue their participation in a sport when selecting participants.[41] A grantee official said that in reviewing applications from veterans and service members wishing to join an event, they consider the proximity of the applicant to ongoing programs offering the same adaptive sport. The aim is to ensure that veterans participating in the grant-funded event also stay involved in the sport for their ongoing well-being and health. VA officials agreed with this aim and said in the future they may consider grant applications, for example, that propose purchasing adaptive sports supplies and equipment to help benefit veterans over a number of years.

Some Grantees Said that No-Shows by Veterans Registered for an Activity Is Problematic

Some grantee officials who we interviewed spoke of a high incidence of veteran no-shows at adaptive sports activities and events as an impediment to program success. At one of our site visits—a sports clinic in which 7 of 10 registered participants attended—an official said some veterans may cancel on short notice, which deprives other interested veterans from participating. In addition, the official was concerned that excessive no-shows may mean there are not enough athletes to form teams or hold an effective practice session. Another official said considerable time and money has been lost when veterans register but do not participate. The official said some no-shows are understandable, such as when a veteran's plans are affected by a medical condition. Nonetheless, adaptive sports are about more than athletics and are aimed at strengthening "mind and heart" of participants as well, the official said. Some veterans can be victims of learned helplessness after they return from service, the official said, and goal-setting and an insistence on accountability can counter this. Another official said that while nonattendance of registered athletes at their high-profile summer sports camp is not a problem, it can be an issue at less prominent events, such as weeknight archery training sessions.

Some grantees noted that asking participants to have a financial stake in an event could encourage attendance. For example, one official suggested that registrants pay a refundable deposit of perhaps $250 so that they have some "skin in the game" and event sponsors have greater assurance of their attendance. Another grantee official explained that in her organization's experience, requiring an up-front financial commitment is effective. At a 2013 multi-sport event, about 35 of the registered athletes did not attend, resulting in a huge waste of federal funds and missed opportunities for other veterans, she said. To combat this, the organization required a credit card number from registrants for the 2014 event, and informed them they would be charged the cost of one-night's lodging if they failed to attend without prior notice. Under this policy, she said, 82 of the 84 registrants—98 percent—took part. Another grantee official said that while requesting a deposit of some kind might have merit, it could also cause cash flow difficulties for some veterans. He said some participants in weeknight training sessions have a hard time paying public transit fare, so the additional cost of a refundable deposit might be a barrier to participation.

VA officials confirmed that no-shows are a problem. They explained that while its regulations require that adaptive sports events supported by the grants be free of charge for eligible veterans, having strategies to incentivize attendance for those who register—such as charging for a first night's hotel expenses—are permissible.[42] They also said that they have provided informal guidance to some fiscal year 2014 grant recipients on ways to reduce no-show rates—typically this information has been shared with grantees sponsoring large scale events that involve travel.[43] However, VA has not systematically gathered and disseminated permissible techniques for reducing no-show rates to all of its grantees. According to federal internal control standards, program management is responsible for identifying, analyzing, and responding to risks it faces in achieving program objectives.[44] A systematic effort to gather and disseminate techniques to address the no-show issue would be consistent with this requirement.

CONCLUSION

In fiscal year 2014, VA assumed responsibility for selecting and overseeing grantees under the adaptive sports grant program and, despite challenges, awarded 69 grants supporting a wide variety of adaptive sports opportunities for veterans and members of the armed services with disabilities. Our review indicates that through the first half of fiscal year 2015, grantees were substantially complying with reporting requirements and that site visits to selected grantees have identified opportunities for improvement. Further, VA is amending its quarterly reporting template so that it will require a report of staff time spent on direct personal interaction with participants, and time spent on other matters, as required by program regulations. However, VA's draft monitoring plan does not include a regular schedule for site visits or desk audits, which risks the possibility that none will be performed in some years, or that they will be performed very late in the year. Promising practices in ensuring adequate grantee financial systems and proper use of grant funds include review of a certain number of grantees each year, and irregular scheduling risks the possibility that mismanagement or misuse of grant funds will not be promptly detected.

Finally, a significant no-show factor means that program dollars may not be used to their fullest potential. VA officials are aware of this issue, and have taken some steps to address it. However, they have not systematically gathered or disseminated techniques to reduce the no-show rate. Further attention to this matter could better enable VA and grantees to serve as many eligible veterans as there are slots available in funded activities.

RECOMMENDATIONS FOR EXECUTIVE ACTION

To help ensure the best use of the VA Adaptive Sports Grant program funds, we recommend the Secretary of Veterans Affairs direct the Undersecretary for Public and Intergovernmental Affairs to take the following two actions:

Revise the draft monitoring plan to include guidance on the number and frequency of annual site visits and desk audits.

Systematically gather and disseminate, to all its grantees, techniques that can reduce the no-show rate at funded events.

AGENCY COMMENTS

We provided a draft of this report to the Department of Veterans Affairs for review. We received formal written comments, which are reproduced in appendix II. VA concurred with our conclusions and both of our recommendations. With regard to the first recommendation, VA indicated that it had established a requirement that a minimum of 10 percent of grantees would be subject to site visits and/or desk audits each fiscal year. Regarding the second recommendation, VA stated that the agency plans to systematically gather and disseminate techniques from a variety of sources to reduce no-show rates. VA also provided several technical comments which we incorporated as appropriate.

Daniel Bertoni
Director, Education, Workforce, and Income Security

APPENDIX I: OBJECTIVES, SCOPE AND METHODOLOGY

The objectives of this engagement were to determine (1) how the VA adaptive sports grant program selected grantees to provide adaptive sports programs and activities for veterans and service members with disabilities; (2) how VA monitors grantees' use of funds; and (3) what programs and activities have been supported with fiscal year 2014 funds, and what is known about how veterans and service members with disabilities have benefited from these programs and activities. Our work was limited to program grants using fiscal year 2014 funds, which supported grantee activities that were to take place in fiscal year 2015. Because our audit work began and ended during VA's first year of monitoring grantees, our work on VA's grantee monitoring generally covered the first two quarters of fiscal year 2015—October 2014 through March 2015.[1]

We addressed the first objective in several steps. To determine how VA reviewed and selected fiscal year 2014 adaptive sports grant applications, we reviewed key VA documents—including relevant federal laws, program regulations, VA's fiscal year 2014 Notice of Funding Availability, and application instructions—and interviewed VA officials. We also reviewed relevant grants management criteria, including VA's agency-wide grants management policies[2], and best grants management practices that had been identified by members of the Domestic Working Group.[3] Second, to determine how VA staff followed program policies and key criteria, we reviewed the files of 16 fiscal year 2014 grants and examined available documents such as the grant applications and proposals, proposed budgets, evidence of grantees' financial and administrative capability, VA's scoring of grantee proposals, and the grant agreement. We selected grants based on type of organization, amount of grant funding and geography. We selected grants to ensure that we obtained eight from national, four from regional and four from community-based organizations. We selected all grants valued at $250,000 or more—seven from national organizations, three from regional organizations. We then selected the remaining six sample grants randomly—one from a national organization, one from a regional organization, and all four from community-based organizations. Also, we ensured that selected grantees included representation of different geographic regions. Although this sample size does not allow us to project to the universe of the 69 fiscal year 2014 grants, it is nonetheless a substantial sample, representing $3.7 million, or 46 percent, of the $8 million granted in fiscal year 2014. In addition to our review of the 2014 application process, we reviewed relevant documents and interviewed VA officials regarding changes to the grant application and review process in fiscal year 2015.

To address the second objective, we interviewed VA officials, reviewed relevant VA policy documents and relevant grant oversight criteria, and reviewed selected VA oversight documentation. Specifically, we reviewed VA's standard quarterly report template to ensure it conformed to the reporting requirements contained in program regulations. We also reviewed the quarterly reports for the 16 grants selected as described in the preceding paragraph for the first two quarters of fiscal year 2015—the 3-month periods ending December 31, 2014 and March 31, 2015. We also identified issues that VA had raised with the quarterly reports and, in selected instances, followed up with VA on how its review comments were addressed. We also obtained and reviewed reports of 8 VA site visits that had been conducted by the end of June 2015.

To address the third objective, we obtained data from VA on the types of sports events to be provided by each fiscal year 2014 grantee and interviewed VA program officials; USOC officials who had been involved in administering sub-grants prior to December 2013; and representatives of three veterans service organizations—Disabled American Veterans, The American Legion, and Veterans of Foreign Wars. We also obtained VA data on grantee budgets and proposed activities. We interviewed VA officials about this data and determined that it was sufficiently reliable for our purposes. To obtain further perspectives on the value of adaptive sports for veterans and service members, we attended three adaptive sports events funded through VA grants. We selected them in consultation with VA program officials. Specifically, we selected events that were occurring during our review and also considered regional diversity and travel considerations. The events selected, listed below, did not provide a representative sample of all VA-funded adaptive sports activities.

- February 2015 goalball camp conducted by the U.S. Association of Blind Athletes in Fort Wayne, Indiana;
- March 2015 archery camp conducted by the Rehabilitation Institute of Chicago, in Chicago, Illinois; and
- May 2015 multi-sport event conducted by Bridge II Sports in Chapel Hill and Durham, North Carolina.

At each event, we interviewed event organizers, coaches and trainers and event participants; and observed the events. We also interviewed event organizers prior to or during their events.

APPENDIX II: COMMENTS FROM THE DEPARTMENT OF VETERANS AFFAIRS

DEPARTMENT OF VETERANS AFFAIRS
WASHINGTON DC 20420

September 17, 2015

Mr. Daniel Bertoni
Director
Education, Workforce, and
Income Security Issues
U.S. Government Accountability Office
441 G Street, NW
Washington, DC 20548

Dear Mr. Bertoni:

The Department of Veterans Affairs (VA) has reviewed the Government Accountability Office's (GAO) draft report, ***"ADAPTIVE SPORTS GRANT PROGRAM: VA Has Taken Steps toward Better Grantee Selection and Oversight, but Additional Actions Needed"*** (GAO-15-791). VA agrees with GAO's conclusions and concurs with GAO's recommendations to the Department.

The enclosure specifically addresses GAO's recommendations and provides technical comments on the draft report. VA appreciates the opportunity to comment on your draft report.

Sincerely,

Robert L. Nabors II
Chief of Staff

Enclosure

Department of Veterans Affairs (VA) Response to
Government Accountability Office (GAO) Draft Report
"ADAPTIVE SPORTS GRANT PROGRAM: VA Has Taken Steps toward Better Grantee Selection and Oversight, but Additional Actions Needed"
(GAO-15-791)

<u>GAO Recommendation</u>: To help ensure the best use of the VA Adaptive Sports Grant program funds, GAO recommends the Secretary of Veterans Affairs direct the Undersecretary for Public and Intergovernmental Affairs to take the following two actions:

<u>Recommendation 1</u>: Revise the draft monitoring plan to include guidance on the number and frequency of annual site visits and desk audits.

<u>VA Comment</u>: Concur. As part of the grant monitoring plan, the Department of Veterans Affairs (VA) has implemented a minimum level of ten percent of grantees will have annual site visits and/or desk audits during each fiscal year. VA provided site visit reports to GAO covering 11.6 percent of FY2014 Adaptive Sports Grant (ASG) grants and has conducted additional FY2014 ASG-related site visits and a desk audit since the GAO audit period. VA provided GAO with site visit reports on eight site visits covering nine grants with three grantees' headquarters-level assessments: Disabled Sports USA (DSUSA) – Winter Program, DSUSA – Training & Geographic Programs (HQ), Far West Wheelchair Athletic Association (Valor Games Far West), Paralyzed Veterans of America (PVA, HQ), Two Top Mountain Adaptive Sports Foundation (TTMASF, Event & HQ), U.S. Military Racquetball Federation, USA Hockey, and USMMA Sailing Foundation. Due to the high level of interoperability involved in the ASG Program that includes both the VA Office of National Veterans Sports Programs & Special Events (NVSP&SE) and VA facility interactions with grantees, the rate should always exceed ten percent. In addition, a minimum of 4 percent of grantees will have annual site visit and/or desk audits by the end of the second quarter. This will allow for both targeting higher risk grantees and coverage for adaptive sport activities that normally occur during the winter timeframe.

<u>Recommendation 2</u>: Systematically gather and disseminate, to all its grantees, techniques that can reduce the no-show rate at funded events.

<u>VA Comment</u>: Concur. VA is implementing a program to systematically gather and disseminate to all its grantees, techniques that can reduce the no-show rate at funded events. These techniques come from a variety of sources, including VA and DOD programs for disabled Veterans and disabled members of the Armed Forces, interaction with ASG recipients, partnership activities with participating organizations such as Veterans Service Organizations, and the VA ASG Quarterly Reports. However, the new VA approach is more comprehensive. For example, through coordination with VA Recreation Therapy Services, Blind Rehabilitation Services, and VA Medical Centers, processes are established to facilitate disabled Veteran participation. In addition, the change in ASG focus on travel is part of a programmatic approach to award grants with lower risk of no-show rates that detract effectiveness of funds expended.

End Notes

[1] U.S. Bureau of the Census, 2013 American Community Survey.

[2] The program was initially authorized by the Veterans' Benefits Improvement Act of 2008, Pub. L. No. 110-389, Title VII, 122 Stat. 4145, 4180-85. It was temporarily extended in

September 2013 by the Department of Veterans Affairs Expiring Authorities Act of 2013, Pub. L. No. 113-37, § 2(b), 127 Stat. 523, and was subsequently reauthorized in December 2013 by the VA Expiring Authorities Extension Act of 2013, Pub. L. No. 113-59, § 5, 127 Stat. 658-659.

[3] See Pub. L. No. 113-59, § 5(e). Section 5(d) of the law authorizes appropriations for the program through fiscal year 2015.

[4] Pub. L. No. 113-59, § 5(f).

[5] VA awarded grants in September 2014 using fiscal year 2014 dollars. These grants supported grantee activities that were to take place in fiscal year 2015. For purposes of this report, we refer to these as fiscal year 2014 grants.

[6] National Governing Bodies are organizations that oversee all aspects of their sport and are responsible for training, competition, and development of their sports. Both the appellations "Paralympic" and "adaptive sports" can be used when referring to recreational sports for those with a physical or visual disability. However, Paralympic can also refer to elite-level competition. For simplicity, this report uses the term adaptive sports.

[7] From 2008 through September 30, 2013, the law designated United States Paralympics, Inc. as the grantee to whom VA was authorized to award funds. United States Paralympics, Inc. is a division of the USOC. However, as we reported in 2012, when VA was preparing its first grant agreement, it was informed that USOC had dissolved United States Paralympics, Inc. as a separate entity and that it had been superseded by the Paralympics Division of the USOC. To ensure grants were used as provide under the law, VA reported that it awarded them directly to USOC. Subsequently, a statutory amendment enacted in September 2013 provided that the USOC, rather than United States Paralympics, Inc., was to be the recipient of any grant funds awarded. Pub. L. No. 113-37, § 2(b), 127 Stat. 523. USOC is a non-profit organization that is responsible for training, entering, and funding U.S. teams for the Olympic and Paralympic games. The organization also has a well-established history of providing adaptive sports opportunities for people with disabilities.

[8] GAO, Veterans Paralympics Program: Improved Reporting Needed to Ensure Grant Accountability, GAO-12-703 (Washington D.C.: July 2012).

[9] One of the recommendations pertained to VA's review of the USOC's monitoring plan, and is no longer relevant.

[10] See 38 C.F.R. pt. 77.

[11] The Office of Management and Budget (OMB) is responsible for developing government-wide grant guidance to ensure grants are managed properly and the grant funds are spent in accordance with applicable laws and regulations. In December 2013, OMB consolidated its grants management guidance into a single document, titled Uniform Administrative Requirements, Cost Principles, and Audit Requirements (Uniform Guidance), and published it in part 200 of title 2 of the Code of Federal Regulations. OMB guidance is applicable to all grant programs and provides policies to be followed by the grant-making agencies. These agencies then codify OMB's guidance into their own grant regulations, making them binding on grantees. All of the grant-making agencies, including VA, adopted the Uniform Guidance for grants issued after December 26, 2014. For purposes of our review, the government-wide grant requirements for VA grantees were found at 38 C.F.R. parts 41 and 43.

[12] Grants for Adaptive Sports Programs for Disabled Veterans and Disabled Members of the Armed Forces, 79 Fed. Reg. 37,211 (July 1, 2014).

[13] VA officials told us that they sought in various ways to ensure that potential applicants were aware of the grant program, in addition to issuing the Notice of Funding Availability. For

example, officials told us they notified hundreds of organizations that had made inquiries about adaptive sport in recent years, coordinated and communicated with Veteran Service Organizations, relevant state agencies, and organizations such as the American Therapeutic Recreation Association.

[14] The panel consisted of three VA reviewers, including a rehabilitation therapy specialist, a health systems specialist who is also an adaptive paddle boarding instructor, and a public affairs officer with experience in community outreach. In some cases, a VA program official substituted for a panel member when, for example, a panel member had a conflict of interest involving an applicant.

[15] The Notice of Funding Availability stated that the ranked scores of applications would be used as the primary basis for selection. However, VA officials also explained that other considerations were permissible. These include selecting applicants that would be operating activities in locations with a large population of disabled veterans, and ensuring the appropriateness of proposed grantee expenditures.

[16] If VA had not obligated available fiscal year 2014 funds by September 30, 2014, those funds would have expired and no longer been available for new obligations. Therefore, VA officials explained that it was important that it selected grantees by September 30, 2014—the last day of fiscal year 2014.

[17] The SF-424 Application for Federal Assistance is used by Grants.gov as a standard federal grant application form. It has been approved by OMB as OMB 4040-004.

[18] 38 U.S.C. § 521A(d)(4)(A)(ii). For grants awarded for adaptive sports opportunities taking place during subsequent fiscal years, the administrative cost limit will be 5 percent. 38 U.S.C. § 521A(d)(4)(A)(iii).

[19] In fiscal year 2014, VA encouraged applicants to submit the questionnaire, but said that they could not mandate its use because it was not yet an established, VA-approved grant application document at the time when paperwork requirements were finalized. Since that time, VA's Office of Finance has approved the use of this form, and the Adaptive Sports Grant Program has opted to require it as a part of grant applications in fiscal year 2015 and moving forward.

[20] While some grant applications lacked evidence of an intention to observe the 7.5 percent limit on administrative expenses, all grant agreement documents included this limit as a standard feature.

[21] In fiscal year 2015, VA received 178 grant applications by the due date of May 26, 2015. VA announced the award of 86 grants on September 15, 2015.

[22] Department of Veterans Affairs Adaptive Sports Grant Application, VA Form 10096, Feb. 2015.

[23] See 2 C.F.R. § 200.328.

[24] 38 C.F.R. § 77.16(a) and (b). Grantees' annual reports pertaining to fiscal year 2014 grants are due by the end of November 2015. Consequently, we were not able to obtain or review these reports.

[25] Regular reporting of relevant, reliable, and timely information is necessary for an entity to run and control its operations according to Standards for Internal Control in the Federal Government and the federal government's internal control framework. Internal controls provide reasonable assurance that, in the federal government, the following objectives are being achieved: effective and efficient operations, reliable financial reporting, and compliance with applicable laws and regulations. Internal controls help government program managers achieve desired results through effective stewardship of public resources. For more information about federal government internal controls, see Standards

for Internal Control in the Federal Government. GAO/AIMD-00-21.3.1 (Washington, D.C.: Nov. 1999) and Office of Management and Budget (OMB) Circular A123 Revised.

[26] The program's statutory authorization requires annual reports. 38 U.S.C. § 521A(j). Under the Uniform Guidance, agencies may require performance reports as frequently as once a quarter. 2 C.F.R. § 200.328(b)(1). VA requires adaptive sports grantees to report quarterly, submitting the reports no later than 30 days after the close of a fiscal quarter. See 38 C.F.R. § 43.40(b)(1). For the first quarter (October-December 2014), the submission deadline was January 30, 2015. For the second quarter (January-March 2015), the submission deadline was April 30, 2015.

[27] According to VA's program regulations, the information requirements for the annual and quarterly reports are the same. 38 C.F.R. § 77.16(b).

[28] GAO-12-703. GAO recommended that grantees include only grant funds in expenditure reports, and that a consistent methodology be provided to grantees for counting program activities and participants.

[29] 38 C.F.R. § 77.16(a)(1).

[30] The regulations (38 C.F.R. § 77.16) detail the requirements for information in annual reports; and that quarterly reports should have the same types of information.

[31] While VA included locations for some activities in grantees' report templates, this was not consistently done.

[32] GAO, Grants to State and Local Governments: An Overview of Federal Funding Levels and Selected Challenges, GAO-12-1016 (Washington, D.C.: Sept. 25, 2012).

[33] In May 2015, we visited Valor Games Southeast, in Chapel Hill and Durham, North Carolina. While Bridge II Sports was the VA grantee operating the event, other VA adaptive sports grantees partnered with it. For example, a representative of U.S. Rowing conducted the indoor rowing event.

[34] GAO-12-1016.

[35] GAO/AIMD-00-21.3.1.

[36] Domestic Working Group Grant Accountability Project, Guide to Opportunities for Improving Grant Accountability, October 2005. Chaired by the Comptroller General of the United States, the Domestic Working Group consists of federal, state and local audit organizations. The working group members identified grant accountability issues, including agency monitoring of grantees; and promising agency practices to address these issues.

[37] GAO/AIMD-00-21.3.1.

[38] For each of the 2 grants, the grantee submitted a blank first-quarter report, because it had not yet conducted any activities, nor had it spent any grant funds. In their second-quarter reports, both grantees reported planning and outreach activities, but no expenditures.

[39] These site visits were to 7 VA grantees. One grantee received 2 VA site visits, covering 3 grants.

[40] As we reported in 2012, VA and USOC hired a contractor to conduct a study on the effects of adaptive sports on rehabilitation and reintegration of veterans and service members into the community (GAO-12-703). However, according to VA officials, the contractor's work did not meet objectives and the contract expired with no acceptable deliverable. VA provided guidance to grant applicants in 2014 indicating that the program is not authorized to fund adaptive sports research, and as such, research is not an authorized activity for grantees.

[41] Because funded adaptive sports activities may have limited available slots, participants may have to submit an application to and be selected by grantees.

[42] Program regulations state that grantees may not charge participants a fee for providing the adaptive sports activities outlined in their grant application. 38 C.F.R. § 77.3(d). However

grantees may charge participants for activities or services that were not outlined in the grant agreement.

[43] VA officials also said that the desire to improve attendance is one reason, in evaluating applications for fiscal year 2015 grants, they may emphasize funding for equipment that veterans and service members could use in their communities over funding for travel to remote events.

[44] For more information about federal government internal controls, see Standards for Internal Control in the Federal Government. GAO-14-704G (Washington, D.C., September 2014).

End Notes for Appendix I

[1] Previously, VA awarded a grant to USOC, which sub-granted funds to organizations providing adaptive sports opportunities. USOC was responsible for selecting and monitoring sub-grantees.

[2] VA's agency-wide grants management policies are documented in VA's Financial Policy Volume X.

[3] Guide to Opportunities for Improving Grant Accountability, Domestic Working Group Grant Accountability Project, October 2005. Chaired by the Comptroller General of the United States, the Domestic Working Group consists of federal, state and local audit organizations. The working group members identified grant accountability issues, including agency monitoring of grantees; and promising agency practices to address these issues.

In: Adaptive Sports …
Editor: Devin Morales

ISBN: 978-1-63484-916-6

Chapter 2

U.S. PARALYMPICS INTEGRATED ADAPTIVE SPORTS PROGRAM: ANNUAL REPORT TO CONGRESS [2015]*

Office of National Veterans Sports Programs and Special Events

OUR MISSION

The Office of National Veterans Sports Programs and Special Events' (NVSP&SE) provides rehabilitative opportunities for eligible Veterans to improve independence, wellbeing and quality of life through adaptive sport, recreation and art therapy programs.

NVSP&SE does this by managing six national events and awarding grants to provide adaptive sports opportunities for disabled Veterans and disabled members of the Armed Forces.

---

* This is an edited, reformatted and augmented version of report issued by the U.S. Department of Veterans Affairs, October 21, 2015.

VISION

Since its inception, NVSP&SE has been dedicated to providing disabled Veterans with constructive and positive relationship-building programs that facilitate their entry into VA's system of rehabilitative care. The experience of the disabled Veterans and members of the Armed Forces is founded on and guided by staff that faithfully embraces VA's I-CARE core values of Integrity, Commitment, Advocacy, Respect and Excellence.

EXECUTIVE SUMMARY

The Office of NVSP&SE provides opportunities for disabled Veterans and disabled members of the Armed Forces to participate in rehabilitative sport and art therapy programs. Veterans may suffer from post-traumatic stress disorder or traumatic brain injuries; others have lost limb(s) or mobility, or have become blind or visually impaired; while some deal with a combination of injuries or conditions.

As the therapeutic and competitive sport needs of disabled Veterans and wounded service members becomes more defined, there is an equally increasing need to promote and highlight the benefits of participating or competing in adaptive sports and the importance of providing those opportunities. VA supports the wellness of Veterans and service members with disabilities and promotes their participation in adaptive sports as a means toward living healthier, happier and more productive lives.

Veterans of all ages can participate in NVSP&SE events – from those recently serving to those who served in World War II, Korea and Vietnam. The place to start is www.va.gov/adaptivesports/The Web site has information on grants, allowances, National rehabilitation special events, videos, and a Sport Club finder to help Veterans locate activities within their communities.

2013 marked a major change in VA's grant program. Under the program's original legislative authority, Public Law 110-389, VA was authorized to award grants only to the United States Olympic Committee's (USOC) U.S. Paralympics Division for an integrated adaptive sports program. In December 2013, Public Law 113-59 modified this legislation by changing the eligibility criteria such that organizations other than the USOC could apply directly to VA for grant funding. Thus, this annual report details the final year of the U.S.

Paralympics Integrated Adaptive Sport Program and transition to the VA Adaptive Sport Grant program.

PROGRAM DESCRIPTIONS, MISSIONS AND HIGHLIGHTS

Paralympic Grant Program

During the reporting period, VA awarded $8 million in grant funding to the U.S. Olympic Committee (USOC) to manage U.S. Paralympics programs and to award subgrants to Paralympic Sport Clubs, colleges and universities, hospitals, Veteran and military organizations, and other qualifying recipients nationwide. This served to enhance and expand the local community-based Paralympic and adaptive sports programs.

Though implementation of grant funded programming was impacted by legislative changes, the U.S. Paralympics administered $6,983,777.71 in grant funds and provided adaptive sports opportunities for 4,415 disabled Veterans and disabled members of the Armed Forces.

Paralympic Assistance Allowance Program

The program provides a monthly assistance allowance to disabled Veterans training in their respective Paralympic sports as authorized by the Veterans' Benefits Improvement Act of 2008 and defined in 38 CFR Part 76. Under this program, VA pays monthly allowances to Veterans with either a service-related or non-service-related disability if they are selected and are actively training or competing in a Paralympic sport for a slot on the United States Paralympics team. Throughout the reporting year, VA awarded a total of $1,167,820.21 in allowance payments to 163 disabled Veterans competing across 23 different Paralympic sports.

National Rehabilitation Special Events

These events promote physical, social, and emotional wellbeing for all Veteran participants by encouraging independence, healthier lifestyles, and maximum performance. Through these programs, the office hosted six national rehabilitative sport and art therapy opportunities to 4,993 Veterans served by VA medical facilities nationwide.

Collaboration and Program Development

These initiatives capitalize on the synergies established through the three core programs and build upon VA and Department of Defense activities to produce complementary therapeutic sport opportunities in line with 38 U.S.C. § 523.

Transition to Public Law 113-59

The reporting period marked a transition from the USOC administered program to the VA Adaptive Sport Grant program. This transition includes changes in the functional relationships and operational environment related to VA, the USOC, and other adaptive sport entities in the United States.

Paralympic Grant Program

1.1. Program Overview

Participating in national, regional, and community-based Paralympic and adaptive sport and rehabilitative programs are essential factors in improving overall health for disabled Veterans and disabled members of the Armed Forces. These programs are critical to improve the health-life plan of Veterans as well as to treat physical, mental and visual impairments. Also, these athletic opportunities assist in reintegrating Veterans back into their communities after the completion of service.

On July 23, 2013, the USOC submitted an application for $8,000,000 in grant funding including sub-awards to 70 community, regional and national partners. VA approved the grant application on Sept. 27, 2013, for a total award of $8,000,000 covering the period September 1, 2013, through September 30, 2014. Additionally, the U.S. Paralympics requested approval to carry over $506,403 of FY12 grant funds returned by a subgrant recipient. VA approved this request bringing the total amount of funding authorized to

$8,506,403. The USOC also requested, and VA approved, an extension to the FY13 grant period of performance to December 31, 2014.

Due to expiring legislative authority and the uncertainty of reauthorization, the U.S. Paralympics did not administer the full grant award. The U.S. Paralympics reported use of $6,983,777.71 in grant funding, leaving a balance of $1,522,625.29 in unused funds. The following details on the Grant Program account for the $6,983,777.71 in grant funds.

Similar to prior applications, the grant award was applied to two funding areas: (1) Grant Programs and (2) USOC Paralympic Programs. As shown in Table 1, approximately $5.8 million was dedicated to grant programs, which accounts for 83 percent of the grant. Also, approximately $1.2 million was allocated for USOC operated programs.

Funding Area	Total Dollars
Grant Programs	$5,785,109.71
USOC Paralympic Programs	$1,198,668.00
TOTAL	**$6,983,777.71**

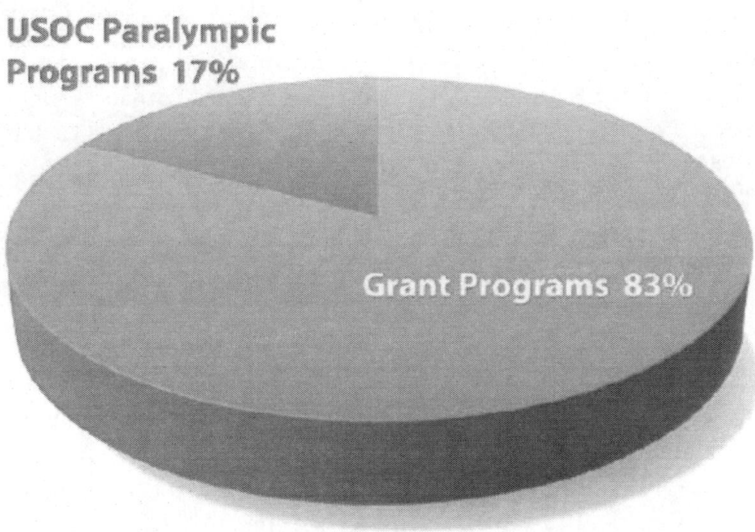

Figure 1. Grant Award by Funding Area.

1.2. Grant Program

The grant program provides funding assistance to national, regional, and community-based organizations that provide Paralympic and adaptive sport opportunities to disabled Veterans and disabled members of the Armed Forces. Organizations applied for grants in the following program areas that provide a multi-level approach for ensuring athletic opportunities are available across a variety of sports and competitive levels:

1) Community, Regional and National Partnerships
2) Sport Development
3) Valor Games Series
4) Program Development
5) Regional Competitions / Conference

Appendix A provides a list of the organizations that received Paralympic subgrants from USOC with FY 2013 funding. For details on the FY 2013 grant award funding for this program, see *Figure 2: Grant Subaward By Funding Area.*

Community, Regional and National Partnerships

The Community, Regional and National partners include non-profit organizations, parks and recreation departments, veterans service organizations, colleges and universities and other organizations that demonstrate the fundamentals necessary for high-quality, sustainable programs serving disabled Veterans and disabled members of the Armed Forces. These partners offer sport camps, clinics, competitions and ongoing programming at select locations across the country. During this grant period, the U.S. Paralympics awarded up to 34 subgrants ranging from $14,750 to $500,000 to partner organizations.

Sport Development

Under these partnerships, USOC affiliated National Governing Bodies (NGBs) and High Performance Management Organizations (HPMOs) provide motivation, sport-specific instruction, skill development and camaraderie for disabled Veterans and disabled members of the Armed Forces. These partnerships foster the development of an infrastructure necessary to prepare Veteran athletes for the highest levels of competition. The U.S. Paralympics awarded up to 19 subgrants to NGBs and HPMOs ranging in amounts from $15,000 to $500,000 during the grant performance period.

Valor Games Series

The Valor Games Series provides multi-day and multi-sport events in targeted areas and provides opportunities for Veteran athletes to compete and advance in their sport. The Valor Games are hosted by community partners and support the identification and eligibility for Veteran participation in the monthly assistance allowance program, emerging athlete camps, and select competitions. These events engage Veterans and connect them to local resources in their communities to advance their training objectives.

Program Development

The program development partnerships are designed to facilitate the development of synergies between community-based partners and VA entities in areas where relationships and programming did not previously exist. These grants are intended to create, expand and/or continue Paralympic sport or physical activity projects for disabled Veterans and disabled members of the Armed Forces in collaboration with a partner community-based organization. Subgrants are intended to accomplish any or all of the following:

1) development of a collaborative relationship between a VA entity and a community-based organization;
2) development of programming in a new geographic area where none exists;
3) development of new programming that has the opportunity to make a significant impact on the lives of disabled Veterans and disabled members of the Armed Forces.

Regional Competitions/Conference

Grant funds were also used to support regional competitions and a national conference on adaptive sports hosted by the United States Association of Blind Athletes. Competitions help identify Veteran athletes capable of excelling in a particular sport for coaching and mentoring. The national adaptive sports conference, held Sept. 15-18, 2014, in Colorado Springs, CO, provided adaptive sports professionals from across the country with educational opportunities and experience developing several Paralympic sports for visually impaired Veterans including judo, rowing, biathlon and more.

Funding Area	Total Dollars
Community, Regional, and National Partnerships	$2,227,183.65
Sport Development	$2,349,875.91
Valor Games Series	$772,671.37
Program Development	$116,196.43
Regional Competitions / Conference	$319,182.35
TOTAL SUBAWARDS	$5,785,109.71

Figure 2. Grant Subaward by Funding Area.

1.3. USOC Paralympic Programs

The USOC Paralympic programs funding was divided into four distinct areas: (1) Technical Assistance and Grant Monitoring, (2) Outreach and Awareness, (3) Sport Performance Development, and (4) Direct Program Staffing (see *Figure 3*).

Grant funded activities provided a variety of sport opportunities for disabled Veterans, ranging from instructional camps and clinics to competitive events. The following table identifies the type of activities for each quarter during the fiscal year. Note: the number of Veterans participating in activities includes individuals attending multiple events, for a total of 7,900 sport opportunities. To calculate the number of unique Veterans participating in these opportunities for the reporting period, we removed duplicate Veteran name / zip codes to obtain a unique Veteran count of 4,415.

USOC Sport Activities

Veterans may participate in multiple sport activities at the local, regional, national, and international levels. These sports include:

Air Pistol
Goalball
Snowboarding
Air Rifle

PROGRAM AREA	TOTAL DOLLARS
Technical Assistance & Grant Monitoring	$238,215
Outreach and Awareness	$73,317
Sport Performance Development	$227,865
Direct Program Staffing	$659,270
TOTAL USOC PROGRAMS	**$1,198,668**

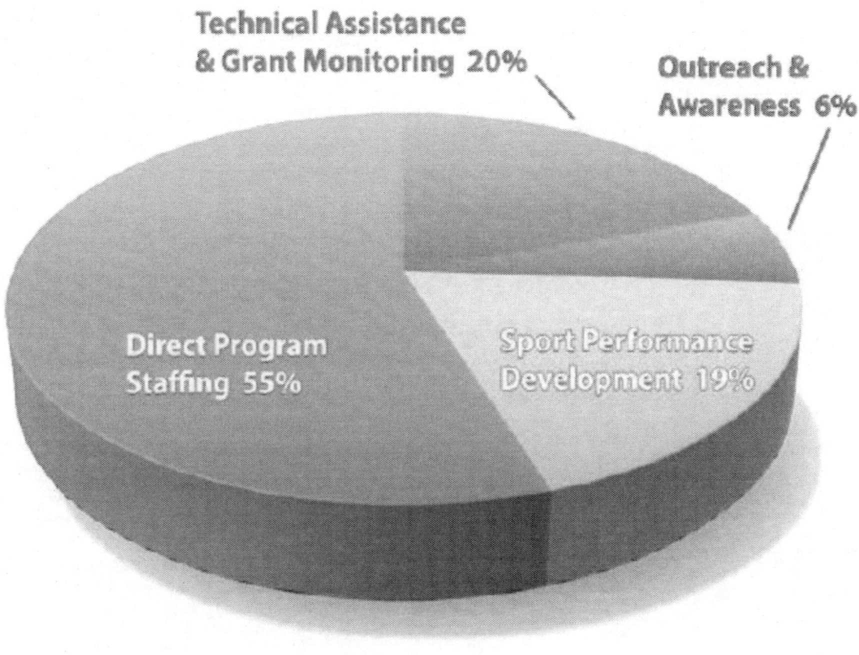

Figure 3. Total Funding by USOC Program Area.

Golf
Surfing
Alpine Skiing
Hiking
Swimming
Aquatics

Ice/Sled Hockey
Table Tennis
Archery
Judo
Tennis
Basketball
Kayaking
Track and Field
Biathlon
Nordic/Cross Country
Skiing Transitions
Boccia
Paddle Boarding
Volleyball
Camping
Paratriathlon
Water Skiing
Canoeing/Va'a
Powerlifting
Weightlifting
Climbing
Power Soccer
Wheelchair Basketball
Curling
Racquetball
Wheelchair/Quad Rugby
Cycling/Handcycling
Rowing
Wheelchair Racing
Equestrian
Running
Wheelchair Softball
Fishing
SCUBA
Wheelchair Soccer
Fencing
Sailing

Wheelchair Tennis
Fitness
Shooting

1.4. Grant Oversight

VA and the U.S. Paralympics have continued to perform grant monitoring and oversight responsibilities in accordance with the July 2012 General Accounting Office report (GAO-12-703) "Veterans Paralympic Program - Improved Reporting Needed to Ensure Grant Accountability."

During the reporting period, the U.S. Paralympics established guidelines for grant oversight and monitoring activities that included site visits, desk audits and/or financial reviews of subgrant recipients. U.S. Paralympics also established risk assessment indicators to track subgrant progress toward achieving deliverables, including timely and accurate reporting, solid communication and solid results. The risk assessment indicators resulted in U.S. Paralympics performing financial and program desk reviews of 10 subgrant recipients.

As previously indicated in this report, this marked the final year of the U.S. Paralympics Integrated Adaptive Sport Program and necessitated internal controls for grant close out and record retention. For subgrant recipients, the close out process included completion of all deliverables, finalization of all obligations, and accounting for all grant funds. To coordinate this process, the U.S. Paralympics developed a detailed expenditure tracking tool for sub-recipient programs. This tool enabled accurate tracking of grant deliverables and spend plans to ensure full accounting and closeout of grant funds. All records associated with the U.S. Paralympics and subgrant awards are to be retained for a minimum of three years.

In addition to the USOC oversight activities, VA grant management specialists conducted visits to the USOC offices in Colorado Springs, CO, to review record keeping and participate in grant monitoring reviews. These included reviewing subgrantee compliance with deliverables, budget, level of participation and other performance measures. VA grant management specialists also reviewed USOC quarterly reports and provided ongoing feedback regarding deliverables.

PARALYMPIC MONTHLY ASSISTANCE ALLOWANCE PROGRAM

2.1. Allowance Overview

The program provides a monthly assistance allowance to disabled Veterans training in their respective sports as authorized by the *Veterans' Benefits Improvement Act of 2008* and defined in 38 CFR Part 76. Through the program, VA and USOC support disabled Veteran athletes who are in a full-time, coached program. During this reporting period, USOC and National Governing Bodies (NGB) in Paralympic sports further developed Paralympic allowance standards, created new partnerships and programs to expand opportunities for Veterans, and increased the number of Veterans on the emerging and national teams. In addition, VA and USOC established programs to help disabled military athletes transition to the allowance and enable opportunities to participate in new Paralympic sports. The current IPC certified Paralympic sports are shown in Appendix C.

Throughout the reporting year, VA awarded $1,167,820.21 in allowance payments to 163 disabled Veterans competing across 23 different Paralympic sports.

In addition, VA coordinated with numerous government offices, Olympic Committees, Paralympic Committees, and other adaptive sport entities to establish partnerships for enabling the monthly assistance allowance in United States Commonwealths and Territories. These activities were subsequently incorporated into the allowance program through Public Law 113-59, the *VA Expiring Authorities Extension Act of 2013*.

NATIONAL REHABILITATION SPECIAL EVENTS

3.1. Overview

VA's adaptive sport and recreation therapy programs can be traced to the rehabilitation of war injured Veterans following World War II. In 1981, which the United Nations proclaimed as the International Year of Disabled Persons, VA hosted the first *National Veterans Wheelchair Games* to provide a competitive outlet for Veterans who use wheelchairs for sports and now has grown to be the largest annual rehabilitation and wheelchair sports competition in the world. In 1985, VA hosted the first *National Veterans Golden Age Games* to improve the health and wellness of Veterans age 55 and older.

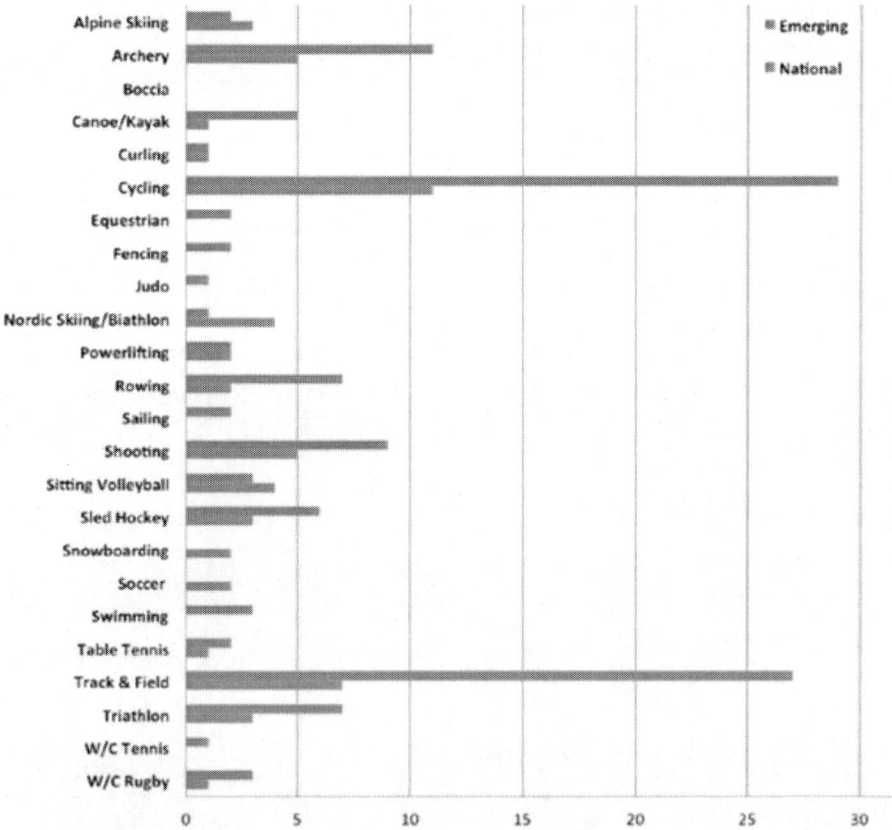

Figure 5. Total Number of National Team and Emerging Athletes by Paralympic Sport.

In 1987, VA launched the *National Disabled Veterans Winter Sports Clinic* to teach adaptive winter sports to Veterans receiving care at VA medical facilities. In 1989, VA held its first *National Veterans Creative Arts Competition and Festival* as a showcase for the healing power of art, music, drama and dance. The competition attracts thousands of Veterans from VA facilities nationwide with the top medal winners being invited to showcase their work at the annual Festival. In 2008, VA piloted the *National Veterans Summer Sports Clinic* to introduce recently-injured Veterans to adaptive sports as part of their rehabilitation. That same year, an adaptive golfing program developed at the Iowa City VA Medical Center - the *National Veterans TEE Tournament* - became one of VA's National rehabilitation special events.

These programs provide a patient-centered approach to rehabilitation and community reintegration, and encourages Veterans to redefine their capabilities, establish rehabilitative goals, and re-discover their potential in a therapeutic environment. Through these annual events, Veterans find increased confidence, self-esteem, independence and a higher quality of life.

Each event is made possible through the collaborative efforts of VA medical facilities, National sponsors, and community partner organizations. During the reporting period, the Office hosted the following National events and provided rehabilitative sport and creative arts therapy opportunities to 4,993 Veterans:

NATIONAL EVENTS

Event	Date (2014)	Location	Veterans
National Disabled Veterans Winter Sports Clinic	3/29 - 4/4	Snowmass, CO	290
National Veterans Golden Age Games	6/28 - 7/2	Fayetteville, AR	635
National Veterans Wheelchair Games	8/12 - 8/17	Philadelphia, PA	550
National Veterans TEE Tournament	9/8 - 9/12	Iowa City, IA	185
National Veterans Summer Sports Clinic	9/7 - 9/12	San Diego, CA	125
National Veterans Creative Arts Festival	10/27 - 11/2	Milwaukee, WI	3,208 - Competition 147 - Festival

Collaboration and Program Development

During this period, VA and USOC identified multiple opportunities for collaboration and program development. These efforts led to enhancements in both the Paralympic Grant and Monthly Assistance Allowance Programs.

4.1. Enhancing VA and Community Partnerships

The USOC coordinated with 15 VA Medical Centers and subgrant recipients to develop joint, ongoing programming for disabled Veterans and disabled members of the Armed Forces in their communities. A total of 460 disabled Veterans benefited from these collaboration programs. Through these efforts, Veterans are able to integrate into their communities for adaptive sport services. Additionally, NVSP&SE took steps to conduct outreach to veterans' organizations, universities, non-profit groups and other adaptive sport providers to enhance awareness of adaptive sport programming for disabled Veterans and disabled members of the Armed Forces.

4.2. Support for Camps and Competitions

Under the FY2013 grant, the USOC provided support to 13 camps and competitions serving 343 disabled Veterans and injured service members. These include:

- Empire State Games, Feb. 6-19
- Elite Throws Camp, April 7-13
- Texas Regional Games, April 11-13
- Great Lakes Adaptive Sports
- Association Gateway to Gold, April 27
- Desert Challenge Camp, May 5-11
- Gateway Games, May 16-18
- Bend Camp, May 23-26
- Endeavor Tri Camp, June 3-9
- Great Lakes Adaptive Sports Association Games, June 13-14
- Bay Area Gateway to Gold, July 3
- Development Archery Camp, July 21-25
- Southern California Gateway to Gold, July 31
- Warrior Games, Sept. 26-Oct. 4

4.3. Outreach

The Paralympic Winter Games were held in Sochi March 7 – 16, 2014, during the grant-funded period. The USOC and VA worked collaboratively to promote the Games, with much emphasis on the Veteran athletes competing in the Games. These efforts resulted in numerous media placements including *The New York Times*, *Men's Health, Field and Stream*, and *Sports Illustrated Kids* among others. Momentum from the Sochi Winter Games led to multiple speaking engagements, mentor visits and media opportunities including the PBS Ice Warriors documentary on sled hockey and the NBC broadcast of the Sochi gold medal sled hockey game reaching millions of viewers. VA and USOC also worked collaboratively to promote grant-funded events on social media sites such as Facebook and Twitter and highlight these events on the USOC Sport Club Finder website.

The USOC developed new marketing materials for the Gateway to Gold program, which is a talent identification program to introduce athletes to the pipeline for the U.S. Paralympic Team. These marketing materials included images of Veteran athletes and text indicating that the program is open to Veterans and service members with physical disabilities.

Another component of outreach included development and training for grant sub-recipients. The USOC implemented a number of steps to ensure sub-recipients understood and complied with federal grant reporting policies. These included hosting several webinars on best practices and other relevant topics, issuing a monthly grant newsletter and releasing "hot item" e-mails to address timely reporting and deliverable requirements.

VA Adaptive Sports Program Web site

The Web site, http://www.va.gov/adaptivesports/, provides users with engaging (both visual and informational), dynamic content about Paralympic and adaptive sports. The Web site includes features such as a comprehensive overview of the benefits of adaptive sports, sports by disability, information about the grant program and training allowances, success stories, and an Adaptive Sports Club Finder. The capabilities have been expanded, including more details on selected new Paralympic grant-related programs like the Valor Games and other Paralympic and adaptive sport publications.

Social Media

TWITTER:
www.twitter.com/VAAdaptiveSport

FLICKR:
www.flickr.com/photos/VeteransAffairs

FACEBOOK:
www.facebook.com/VAAdaptiveSports

YOUTUBE:
www.youtube.com/DeptVetAffairs

Promotional Videos

NVSP&SE is developing promotional videos that highlight our national events. These inspirational and informational messages are part of our ongoing mission to promote participation and awareness of the numerous opportunities available to disabled Veterans and disabled Servicemembers.

Social Media

NVSP&SE has expanded our social media capabilities, utilizing various outlets such as Twitter, Facebook, Instagram, and more to maintain an ongoing source of current information on Paralympic and adaptive sports for disabled Veterans.

Transition to Public Law 113-59

During this period, the passage of Public Law 113-59 in December 2013 changed the functional relationships and operational environment related to VA, the USOC, and other adaptive sport entities in the United States. These changes impacted the full spectrum of VA interaction with the adaptive sports communities.

5.1. VA Program Management Infrastructure Development

P.L. 113-59 required immediate VA assumption for management of the new grants for adaptive sports programs for disabled Veterans and disabled members of the armed forces. Because VA requires regulations for all grant programs, a formal regulation was required to be approved by VA and the Office of Management and Budget prior to publication in the Federal Register before any FY2014 Notice of Funding Availability (NOFA) could be released.

Through cooperative efforts VA completed and published 38 CFR Part 77, Adaptive Sports Programs for Disabled Veterans and Disabled Members of the Armed Forces, in the Federal Register on July 1, 2014. The following week, VA published the FY2014 Adaptive Sports Grant NOFA, received 161 Adaptive Sports Grant (ASG) applications, established all tools and processes to evaluate these applications, and awarded 69 grants worth $8 million to 65 adaptive sport entities by the end of September 2014.

5.2. Resource Allocation

To manage the FY2014 ASG program, the VA created diverse tools and processes for all new duties and responsibilities associated with the program. Due to the immediate transition during the fiscal year, VA implemented the ASG program with existing manpower, budget, and other resources. This implementation method enabled the full $8 million authorized to be allocated for adaptive sports grants.

5.3. Paralympic Sport Development

During the reporting period, VA increased outreach to National Governing Bodies in adaptive sports under consideration for International Paralympic Committee (IPC) certification as Paralympic sports. For example, VA worked with USA Badminton, USA Bobsled/Skeleton and USA Taekwondo to develop the infrastructure for their sports with involvement of disabled Veterans as core to these initiatives. In addition, VA worked with US Soccer and BlazeSports America in an initiative to develop pipelines in 7-a-Side Soccer for disabled Veterans with TBI and to create the infrastructure to develop a national 5-a-Side Soccer for blind and visually impaired athletes with the focus on disabled Veterans. The IPC has certified 7-a-Side Soccer as a Paralympic sport.

5.4. United States Commonwealth and Territories

Passage of P.L. 113-59, gave VA authority to engage Paralympic and adaptive sport entities in American Samoa, Guam, the Commonwealth of the Northern Mariana Islands, Puerto Rico, and the U.S. Virgin Islands to enable equal involvement in VA's Adaptive Sports Grant and Paralympic allowance programs. During FY2014, VA developed partnerships to enable full implementation with the American Samoa National Olympic Committee (ASNOC); the Puerto Rico Paralympic Committee; the Northern Mariana Amateur Sports Association; and the National Paralympic Committee, U.S. Virgin Islands, each of which are the Paralympic sport authorities in their respective jurisdictions. The results included establishing the basis for activating Paralympic allowance programs in Puerto Rico and the U.S. Virgin Islands and for ASNOC applying for and being awarded an FY2014 Adaptive Sports Grant to establish the first-ever adaptive sports programs for disabled Veterans in American Samoa. VA also interacted with both governmental and private entities both in Guam or with chapters in Guam to develop adaptive sport initiatives; these entities include the Guam National Olympic Committee. However, these initiatives did not achieve the same levels of success as elsewhere.

5.5. Professional Therapeutic Sport Communities

Although some partnerships existed, VA expanded its direct coordination with the professional therapeutic adaptive sport communities in the United States to enhance the adaptive sports grant, Paralympic allowance, and other VA programs. For example, VA worked with the America Therapeutic Recreation Association to disseminate information on the new Adaptive Sports Grant program throughout the national recreation therapy community. VA met with the Amputee Coalition of America and developed plans and initiatives to cooperate through the full spectrum of adaptive sports activities for Veterans with amputations or facing amputations. In some areas, VA began a more comprehensive approach, such as establishing partnership links involving the Blinded Veterans of America, U.S. Association of Blind Athletes, VisionQuest Alliance, Association for Education & Rehabilitation of the Blind and Visually Impaired, the VA Blind Rehabilitation Services, and other adaptive sport entites for enhancing adaptive sports opportunities for blind and visually-impaired Veterans. VA also reinvigorated established partnerships such as with the National Consortium for Physical Education for Individuals with Disabilities in training and technical assistance initiatives in adaptive sports for disabled Veterans.

5.6. More Comprehensive Adaptive Sports for Disabled Veterans

With P.L. 113-59 implementation, VA launched new initiatives in adaptive sports that are not in the realm of Paralympic sports and better consider the needs of disabled Veterans with disabilities not classified under the IPC system, such as PTSD. For example, VA enacted new partnership activities with PATH [Professional Association of Therapeutic Horsemanship] International, the lead national organization in therapeutic riding and equine-assisted therapy. In another initiative, VA partnered with the National Senior Games Association and NSGA is currently implementing adaptive sports into the national Senior Games program.

APPENDIX A: FY2013 PARALYMPIC GRANT RECIPIENTS

Adaptive Action Sports Lummi Island, WA	$25,000	Para snowboard
Adaptive Adventures Lakewood, CO	$45,000	Cycling, Skiing
Adaptive Sports New England Lincoln, NH	$50,000	Fitness, Sailing, Kayaking, Softball, Golf
Bay Area Outreach & Recreation Program Berkeley, CA	$25,000	Cycling, Goalball, Basketball, Kayaking
Buffalo Sabres Foundation Buffalo, NY	$14,750	Sled hockey
Casper Mountain Biathlon Club Casper, WY	$25,000	Biathlon
Central Cross Country Ski Association Verona, WI	$50,000	Cross county skiing
Challenged Athletes Foundation San Diego, CA	$45,000	Multi-sport

ORGANIZATION NAME / LOCATION	GRANT AMOUNT	PARALYMPIC & ADAPTIVE SPORT
COMMUNITY, REGIONAL AND NATIONAL PARTNERSHIPS – $2,227,183.65		
Champions Made From Adversity Augusta, GA	$24,972	Cycling, Archery
City of Boulder Boulder, CO	$15,000	Track and field, Cycling
City of Bryant Bryant, AR	$19,251.69	Archery, Wheelchair basketball
Community Rowing Brighton, MA	$25,000	Rowing
Disabled Athlete Sports Association St. Peters, MO	$17,000	Multi-sport
Disabled Sports USA Rockville, MD	$500,000	Multi-sport
Florida Gulf Coast PVA Tampa, FL	$15,000	Archery
Great Lakes Adaptive Sports Association Lake Forest, IL	$50,000	Track and field, Paratriathlon
Greater Metro Parks Tacoma Tacoma, WA	$20,000	Archery
Injured Marine Semper Fi Fund Oceanside, CA	$35,000	Multi-sport
Loma Linda University Health PossAbilities Loma Linda, CA	$25,000	Para-canoe, Cycling
Lone Star Paralysis Foundation Austin, TX	$125,000	Multi-sport

Appendix A. (Continued)

ORGANIZATION NAME / LOCATION	GRANT AMOUNT	PARALYMPIC & ADAPTIVE SPORT
COMMUNITY, REGIONAL AND NATIONAL PARTNERSHIPS – $2,227,183.65		
Medstar National Rehabilitation Network Washington, DC	$100,000	Archery, Rowing, Wheelchair rugby, Wheelchair basketball, Sailing, Kayaking
Mesa Association of Sports for the Disabled Mesa, AZ	$40,630	Cycling, Kayaking, Track, Field, Archery
National Ability Center Park City, UT	$70,000	Alpine skiing, Snowboarding, Archery, Cycling
National Sports Center for the Disabled Denver, CO	$75,000	Alpine and Nordic skiing, Snowboarding, Para-canoe
New England Nordic Ski Association New Gloucester, ME	$44,604.96	Nordic skiing
Operation Comfort San Antonio, TX	$17,500	Cycling
Paralyzed Veterans of America Washington, DC	$400,000	Cycling, Trapshooting, Bowling
Riekes Center for Human Enhancement Menlo Park, CA	$25,000	Archery, Track and field, Wheelchair rugby
Sanford Medical Center Grand Forks, MN	$14,975	Skiing, Cycling, Archery, Kayaking
SPIRE Institute EVSR Program Geneva, OH	$15,000	Swimming, Running, Handcycling, Wheelchair basketball
Sportable Richmond Adaptive Sports and Recreation Inc. Richmond, VA	$18,500	Rowing, Air rifles, Archery, Tennis
Team River Runner Rockville, MD	$30,000	Paddling, Kayaking

ORGANIZATION NAME / LOCATION	GRANT AMOUNT	PARALYMPIC & ADAPTIVE SPORT
COMMUNITY, REGIONAL AND NATIONAL PARTNERSHIPS – $2,227,183.65		
National Ability Center Park City, UT	$70,000	Alpine skiing, Snowboarding, Archery, Cycling
National Sports Center for the Disabled Denver, CO	$75,000	Alpine and Nordic skiing, Snowboarding, Para-canoe
New England Nordic Ski Association New Gloucester, ME	$44,604.96	Nordic skiing
Operation Comfort San Antonio, TX	$17,500	Cycling
Paralyzed Veterans of America Washington, DC	$400,000	Cycling, Trapshooting, Bowling
Riekes Center for Human Enhancement Menlo Park, CA	$25,000	Archery, Track and field, Wheelchair rugby
Sanford Medical Center Grand Forks, MN	$14,975	Skiing, Cycling, Archery, Kayaking
SPIRE Institute EVSR Program Geneva, OH	$15,000	Swimming, Running, Handcycling, Wheelchair basketball
Sportable Richmond Adaptive Sports and Recreation Inc. Richmond, VA	$18,500	Rowing, Air rifles, Archery, Tennis
Team River Runner Rockville, MD	$30,000	Paddling, Kayaking
University of New Hampshire Northeast Passage Durham, NH	$125,000	Multi-sport
World Sport Chicago Development Program Chicago, IL	$100,000	Multi-sport

Appendix A. (Continued)

ORGANIZATION NAME / LOCATION	GRANT AMOUNT	PARALYMPIC & ADAPTIVE SPORT
COMMUNITY, REGIONAL AND NATIONAL PARTNERSHIPS – $2,227,183.65		
BlazeSports America Atlanta, GA	$45,865.32	Dixie Games
Great Lakes Adaptive Sports Association Deerfield, IL	$20,000	Great Lakes Games
Lone Star Paralysis Foundation San Antonio, TX	$18,317.03	Texas Regional Games
Michigan Sports Unlimited Morley, MI	$37,500	Thunder in the Valley
United States Association of Blind Athletes Colorado Springs, CO	$175,000	Conference
University of Central Oklahoma Edmond, OK	$22,500	Endeavor Games

ORGANIZATION NAME / LOCATION	GRANT AMOUNT
SPORT DEVELOPMENT GRANT: $2,349,875.91	
American Service Member Amateur Sports Boulder, CO	$15,000
Aspen Valley Ski & Snowboard Club Aspen, CO	$500,000
BlazeSports America Decatur, GA	$145,000

ORGANIZATION NAME / LOCATION	GRANT AMOUNT
SPORT DEVELOPMENT GRANT: $2,349,875.91	
Lakeshore Foundation Birmingham, AL	$33,825
National Archery Association of the United States Colorado Springs, CO	$90,000
National Paddling Committee dba USA Canoe Kayak Oklahoma City, OK	$100,000
National Wheelchair Basketball Association Colorado Springs, CO	$120,000
United States Association of Blind Athletes Colorado Springs, CO	$150,000
United States Biathlon Association New Gloucester, ME	$200,000
United States Curling Association Stevens Point, WI	$48,100.66
United States Equestrian Federation Inc. Lexington, KY	$65,409.86
United States Judo Inc. Colorado Springs, CO	$100,000

Appendix A. (Continued)

ORGANIZATION NAME / LOCATION	GRANT AMOUNT
SPORT DEVELOPMENT GRANT: $2,349,875.91	
United States Sailing Association Portsmouth, RI	$80,000
University of Central Oklahoma Edmond, OK	$248,750.72
USA Shooting Colorado Springs, CO	$100,000
USA Table Tennis Colorado Springs, CO	$100,000
USA Triathlon Colorado Springs, CO	$40,143.45
USA Volleyball Colorado Springs, CO	$100,000
USTA Serves White Plains, NY	$113,646.22

ORGANIZATION NAME / LOCATION	GRANT AMOUNT	
VALOR GAMES: $772,671.37		
Bridge II Sports Raleigh, NC	$150,000	Valor Games Southeast
Far West Wheelchair Athletic Association Alameda, CA	$150,000	Valor Games Farwest
San Antonio Sports San Antonio, TX	$147,677.60	Valor Games Southwest
World Sport Chicago Chicago, IL	$175,000	Valor Games Midwest
SPIRE Institute Geneva, OH	$149,993.77	Gold Medal Camp

PROGRAM DEVELOPMENT: $116,196.43	
All Out Adventures Northampton, MA	$14,999
The Center for Individuals with Physical Challenges Tulsa, OK	$15,000
City of Reno Reno, NV	$15,000
Fencers Club New York, NY	$15,000
City of Fort Collins Fort Collins, CO	$15,000
Tennessee Association of Blind Athletes Nashville, TN	$13,000.15

Appendix A. (Continued)

University of Southern Mississippi Hattiesburg, MS	$13,334
Wheelchair Sports Incorporated Wichita, KS	$14,863.28

APPENDIX B: PARTNERSHIPS WITH NATIONAL GOVERNING BODIES

PARALYMPIC SPORT	ORGANIZATION	COMMUNITY
Alpine Skiing	United States Paralympics	Colorado Springs, CO
Archery	USA Archery	Colorado Springs, CO
Badminton	USA Badminton	Colorado Springs, CO
Basketball	National Wheelchair Basketball Association	Colorado Springs, CO
Biathlon	United States Biathlon Association	New Gloucester, ME
Boccia	BlazeSports America, Inc.	Atlanta, GA
Canoe (Va'a) / Kayak	United States Canoe / Kayak	Oklahoma City, OK
Curling	United States Curling Association	Stevens Point, WI
Cycling	United States Paralympics	Colorado Springs, CO
Equestrian	United States Equestrian Federation	Gladstone, NJ
Goalball	United States Association of Blind Athletes	Colorado Springs, CO
Judo	USA Judo	Colorado Springs, CO
Nordic Skiing	United States Paralympics	Colorado Springs, CO
Para-Snowboard	United States Paralympics	Colorado Springs, CO

PARALYMPIC SPORT	ORGANIZATION	COMMUNITY
Paratriathlon	USA Triathlon	Colorado Springs, CO
Powerlifting	United States Paralympic Powerlifting	Edmond, OK
Rowing	United States Rowing	Princeton, NJ
Rugby	Lakeshore Foundation	Birmingham, AL
Sailing	United States Sailing	Portsmouth, RI
Shooting	USA Shooting	Colorado Springs, CO
Sled Hockey	USA Hockey	Colorado Springs, CO
Soccer	United States Soccer Federation	Chicago, IL
Swimming	United States Paralympics	Colorado Springs, CO
Table Tennis	USA Table Tennis	Colorado Springs, CO
Taekwondo	USA Taekwondo	Colorado Springs, CO
Tennis	United States Tennis Association	White Plains, NY
Track and Field	United States Paralympics	Colorado Springs, CO
Volleyball	USA Volleyball	Colorado Springs, CO

Appendix C: Paralympic Sports by Disability Group

PARALYMPIC SPORT	AMPUTEE / DWARFISM/OTHER	BLIND / VISUALLY IMPAIRED	SPINAL CORD INJURY/ PARALYZED /WHEEL-CHAIR USER	TRAUMATIC BRAIN INJURY/CP /STROKE	INTEL-LECTUAL IMPAIR-MENT
Archery	X		X	X	
Badminton			X		
Basketball	X		X		
Boccia				X	

Appendix C. (Continued)

PARALYMPIC SPORT	AMPUTEE / DWARFISM/ OTHER	BLIND / VISUALLY-IMPAIRED	SPINAL CORD INJURY/ PARALYZED /WHEEL CHAIR USER	TRAUMATIC BRAIN INJURY/CP /STROKE	INTEL-LECTUAL IMPAIR-MENT
Canoe/Kayak	X		X	X	
Cycling	X	X	X	X	
Equestrian	X	X	X	X	
Fencing	X		X	X	
Goalball		X			
Judo		X			
Paratriathlon	X	X	X	X	
Powerlifting	X		X	X	
Rowing	X	X	X	X	
Rugby			X		
Sailing	X	X	X	X	
Shooting	X		X	X	
Soccer*				X	
Swimming	X	X	X	X	X
Table Tennis	X		X	X	X
Taekwondo	X				
Tennis	X		X		
Track & Field	X	X	X	X	X
Volleyball	X				
Alpine Skiing	X	X	X	X	
Biathlon	X	X	X	X	
Cross Country Skiing	X	X	X	X	
Curling	X		X	X	
Sled Hockey	X		X	X	
Snowboard	X				

*Soccer exists for Blind/Visually Impaired athletes in international competition, but there is no active U.S. program.

In: Adaptive Sports ...
Editor: Devin Morales

ISBN: 978-1-63484-916-6

Chapter 3

2015 ADAPTIVE SPORTS GRANT RECIPIENTS*

Office of National Veterans Sports Programs and Special Events

SUMMARY: National Organizations: $4,161,707.95; Regional Programs: $2,578,179.27; Community Groups: $1,260,059.06 Awards to adaptive sport organizations headquartered in 31 states plus the District of Columbia 86 total grants; 47 received grants in FY14; 39 are new grant recipients				
NATIONAL ORGANIZATIONS				
STATE	ORGANIZATION	ADAPTIVE SPORTS	AMOUNT	PARTNERS
CA	Challenged Athletes Foundation 9591 Waples St., San Diego, CA 92121	Triathlon, Surfing, Flag Football, Martial Arts, Swimming, Running	$200,000.00	Durham VA, Athletes with Disabilities Network, Valor Games, San Diego District Tennis Assoc., Naval Medical Center San Diego
CA	Disabled Sports Eastern Sierra P.O. Box 7275, Mammoth Lakes, CA 93546	Alpine/Nordic Skiing, Snowboarding, Biathlon, Cycling, Kayaking, Rock Climbing, Fishing, Hiking	$61,800.00	US Forest Service, Mammoth Mountain Ski, Disabled Sports USA, US Paralympics, US Biathlon Assoc., USMC Wounded Warrior Bat. West
CA	Injured Marine Semper Fi Fund P.O. Box 555193	Running, Archery, Shooting, Cycling, Triathlon, Sitting	$125,000.00	Team MPI, Aspen Valley Ski Club, Breckenridge Outdoor Center, Trappers Turn, National

* This is an edited, reformatted and augmented version of report issued by the U.S. Department of Veterans Affairs, 2015.

(Continued)

NATIONAL ORGANIZATIONS				
STATE	ORGANIZATION	ADAPTIVE SPORTS	AMOUNT	PARTNERS
	Camp Pendleton, CA 92055---5193	Volleyball, Wheelchair Basketball, Sled Hockey		Ability Center, USOC
CO	Challenge Aspen81615 P.O. Box 6639, Snowmass Village, CO	Alpine Skiing, Snowboarding	$67,000.00	
CO	National Archery Association (USA Archery) 4065 Sinton Rd., Suite 110 Colorado Springs, CO 80907	Archery	$100,000.00	Texas Regional Games, Endeavor Games, Salt Lake County Adapted Services, VA Summer Sports Clinic
CO	USA Badminton, One Olympic Pl., Colorado Springs, CO 80909---5780	Para---Badminton	$20,700.00	Med Star Health, San Francisco Bay Badminton Club, Endeavor Games, Dixie Games
CO	USA Table Tennis 4065 Sinton Rd., Suite 120, Colorado Springs, CO 80907	Table Tennis	$25,112.11	VA Bronx, San Antonio Table Tennis Club (TTC), Portland TTC, Maryland TTC, South Bend TTC, Las Vegas TTC, Riekes Center for Human Enhancement
CO	USA Triathlon of Colorado 5825 Delmonico Drive, Suite 200 Colorado Springs, CO 80919-2242	Paratriathlon	$77,000.00	Dare 2 Tri, Team RWB, Tri Soldier Project, Team Semper Fi, Wounded Warrior Project, Teams Racing for Veterans, Challenged Athletes
CO	Wheelchair and Ambulatory Sports, USA P.O. Box 621023, Littleton, CO 80162	Air Guns, Shooting	$250,000.00	Denver VA, Tampa VA, Spaulding Adap. Sport, USA Shooting, Fayetteville NC Parks, Sportable, Texas Reg. Paralympics, Turnstone, Great Lakes Adaptive Sport, Adaptive Sport Iowa, AZ Disabled Sports
CO	Breckenridge Outdoor Education Center P.O. Box 697, Breckenridge, CO 80424	Skiing/Snowboarding, Camping, Rafting/Canoeing, Cycling, Climbing	$40,000.00	Denver VA, Adaptive Adventures
CO	National Sports Center for the Disabled 1801 Mile High Stadium Cir., Suite 1500 Denver, CO 80204	Skiing, Biathlon, Paracanoe, Kayak, Stand-up Paddle Board	$107,500.00	Denver VA, Tampa VA, Fort Carson, DAV, DSUSA, Team River Runner

NATIONAL ORGANIZATIONS				
STATE	ORGANIZATION	ADAPTIVE SPORTS	AMOUNT	PARTNERS
CO	National Wheelchair Basketball Assoc. 1130 Elkton Dr., Suite C Colorado Springs, CO 80907	Wheelchair Basketball	$88,252.00	University of Texas at Arlington, Chicago Park District, Naval Medical Center San Diego
CO	Professional Association of Therapeutic Horsemanship (PATH) International 7475 Dakin St., Suite 600 Denver, CO 80221--6920	Therapeutic Riding, Equine Assisted Therapy	$176,275.00	BraveHearts Riding, Calvin Center Horses & Warriors, Hearts & Horses, Horses & Humans Research, Jacob's Ladder Therap. Center, Pony Power Therapies, Ride On Cnt., Horses Help Heroes.
CO	United States Association of Blind Athletes 1 Olympic Plaza Colorado Springs, CO 80909	Goalball, Cycling, Rowing	$130,610.00	VA Blind Rehabilitation Service, US Paralympics, US Rowing/Community Rowing, Inc./Boston University
CO	USA Shooting, 1 Olympic Plaza Colorado Springs, CO 80909	Target Shooting	$100,000.00	
CO	USA Volleyball 4065 Sinton Rd., Suite 200 Colorado Springs, CO 80907	Sitting Volleyball	$110,000.00	S. Texas Volleyball Academy, Triangle Volleyball Club, Univ. Central Oklahoma, 40 Regional Volleyball Associations
DC	Paralyzed Veterans of America 801 18th Street, NW Washington, DC 20006	Handcycling, Fishing, Air Rifle, Pistol, Aquatic sport, Boccia, Trapshooting	$200,000.00	VA Medical Centers, DoD WTUs & WWBns, Mission Bay Aquatic Center, Wheelchair Lacrosse USA
GA	Adaptive Golf Association 94 Lakeshore Circle NE, Marietta, GA 30067	Golf	$110,526.32	Professional Golfers Association, multiple VA Medical Centers
GA	BlazeSports America 1670 Oakbrook Drive, Suite 331 Norcross, GA 30093	Soccer	$64,800.00	Atlanta VA, Oglethorpe University, Wounded Warrior Project
IL	University of Illinois 1901 S. First Street, Suite A, Champaign, IL 61820-7406	Wheelchair racing	$40,000.00	VA Spinal Cord Injury National Program Office
LA	National Senior Games Association 8919	Bowling, Horseshoe,	$89,330.00	VA National Veterans Golden Age Games

(Continued)

NATIONAL ORGANIZATIONS				
STATE	ORGANIZATION	ADAPTIVE SPORTS	AMOUNT	PARTNERS
	World Ministry Ave. Baton Rouge, LA 70810-9006	Shuffleboard		
MD	Project Healing Waters Fly Fishing P.O. Box 695, La Plata, MD 20646--0695	Fly fishing	$298,200.00	Trout Unlimited, International Federation of Fly Fishers, Shepard Center
MD	Disabled Sports USA 451 Hungerford Dr. Suite 100 Rockville, MD 20850	Alpine Skiing, Nordic Skiing, Snowshoeing, Curling, Sled Hockey, Biathlon, Snowboarding	$376,842.11	PSIA---AASI, USA Biathlon, Challenged Athletes of West Virginia, Sports, Arts and Rec. of Chattanooga, Maine Adaptive Sports, Oregon Adaptive Sports
MD	Disabled Sports USA 451 Hungerford Dr. Suite 100 Rockville, MD 20850	Training Adaptive Sport Practitioners and Veterans in Archery, Rock Climbing, Taekwondo, Badminton, Cycling, Kayaking, Fishing, SCUBA	$250,000.00	USA Archery, USA Badminton, USA Taekwondo, Soldiers Undertaking Disabled SCUBA, Project Healing Waters, Northeast Passage
MD	Team River Runner, Inc. 5007 Stone Rd., Rockville, MD 20853	Blind Slalom, Kayak Football, Biathlons, Wilderness Paddling, Family Paddling	$210,697.41	Milwaukee VA, Boise VA, Battle Creek VA, VA New York Harbor, Disabled Sports USA, R4 Alliance, American Canoe Assoc.
NJ	US Rowing Association 2 Wall Street, Princeton, NJ 08540--1513	Adaptive Rowing, Para---Rowing	$299,000.00	VAMCs in Dallas, Denver, Detroit, Durham, Houston, New York, Oklahoma City, Palo Alto, Providence, Puget Sound, San Diego, Univ. of Pacific, PVA, Center/Intrepid, Walter Reed NMMC
NY	USA Boccia Inc.11706 1398 Penataquit Ave., Bay Shore, NY	Boccia	$82,757.00	BlazeSports America
NY	Adaptive Sports Foundation, Inc. P.O. Box 266, Windham, NY 12496	Nordic/Biathlon, Bobsled/Skeleton, Empire State Games, Paracanoe/Kayak	$64,010.00	NY Olympic Development Authority, Capital Region Nordic Alliance, U.S. Paralympics
NY	US Merchant Marine Academy Foundation 300 Steamboat Rd.,	Sailing	$199,390.00	U.S. Sailing

NATIONAL ORGANIZATIONS				
STATE	ORGANIZATION	ADAPTIVE SPORTS	AMOUNT	PARTNERS
	Yocum Sailing Center Kings Point, NY 11024---1699			
OK	University of Central Oklahoma 100 N. University Dr., Edmond, OK 73054	Basketball, Cycling, Archery, Paddling, Shooting, Volleyball, Powerlifting	$139,650.00	Oklahoma City VA, UCO Office of Veteran Student Support
VA	Wounded Warrior Amputee Softball Team 2121 Eisenhower Ave, Suite 300 Alexandria, VA 22314	Softball	$37,256.00	
WI	U.S. Curling Association 5525 Clem's Way, Stevens Point, WI 54482	Curling	$20,000.00	Denver VA
	TOTAL		$4,161,707.95	
		REGIONAL PARTNERS		
STATE	ORGANIZATION	ADAPTIVE SPORTS	AMOUNT	PARTNERS
CA	Central California Adaptive Sports Center P.O. Box 147, Shaver Lake, CA 93664	Skiing, Snowshoeing, Fly fishing, Kayaking, Biking, Hiking, Climbing	$24,510.00	California National Guard: Operation Ready Families
CA	City of Sacramento Department of Parks and Recreation 5735 47th Ave., Sacramento, CA, 95824	Rock climbing, running, cycling	$70,967.00	San Francisco VA, VA Palo Alto, VA Northern California, U.S. Association of Blind Athletes
CA	Far West Wheelchair Athletic Association 3369 Union Ave., San Jose, CA 95124	Archery, Cycling, Biathlon, Field, Powerlifting, Rowing, Swimming, Boccia	$160,000.00	U.S. Coast Guard, VA Palo Alto, San Francisco VA, Paralympic Sport Sacramento, U.S. Biathlon, USA Para Powerlifting, U.S. Rowing Assoc.
CA	Ride 2 Recovery 23679 Calabasas Rd., #420, Calabasas, CA 91302	Adaptive Cycling in Central Florida	$93,389.00	R4 Alliance, Project Rebirth, DSUSA, Walter Reed NMMC, San Diego Naval Medical Center
CO	Adaptive Adventures 1315 Nelson Street Unit 1 Lakewood, CO 80215	Alpine Skiing, Cycling, Watersports, Climbing	$430,000.00	VAMCs in Albuquerque, Chicago, Denver, Hines, Grand Junction, Milwaukee, Tomah, Peterson AFB, Walter Reed

(Continued)

		REGIONAL PARTNERS		
STATE	ORGANIZATION	ADAPTIVE SPORTS	AMOUNT	PARTNERS
				NMMC, Creating Ability, Great Lakes Adaptive, Rehabilitation Institute of Chicago, Steamboat Adaptive, Teton Adaptive
CO	Aspen Valley Ski/Snowboard Club 630 High School Rd., Aspen, CO 81611	Alpine Ski Racing	$40,000.00	Injured Marine Semper Fi Fund, Aspen Ski Co.
FL	Wounded Warriors in Action Foundation 6516 Dolphin Cove Dr., Apollo Beach, FL 33572	Hunting, Fishing, Archery, Skeet/Trap	$36,585.00	Tampa VA, R4 Alliance, Cornell University, BREATH Wellness Foundation
IL	Great Lakes Adaptive Sports Association 400 E Illinois Rd., Lake Forest, IL 60045	Track & Field, Golf, Swimming, Yoga, Great Lakes Regional Games	$41,368.42	Hines VA, Milwaukee VA
MD	Salute to Military Golf Association 14600 Argyle Club Rd., Silver Spring, MD 20906	Golf Instruction & Tournaments	$60,000.00	Purple Heart Foundation, Camp Lejeune, Fort Eustis, Fort Belvoir, Fort Drum
MD	University of Maryland 8400 Baltimore Ave., Suite 200, College Park, MD 20740	Kayaking	$38,797.00	Team River Runner
ME	New England Nordic Ski Association 49 Pineland Drive, Suite 301A New Gloucester, ME 04260	Nordic Skiing, Biathlon, Fly--fishing, Kayaking, Archery	$50,000.00	Brockton VA, Bedford VA, White River Junction VA, Burlington VA, Montachusett Veterans Center, Pineland Farms, US Biathlon Assoc.
ME	Pineland Farms, Inc. 32 Farm View Dr., New Gloucester, ME 04260	WC Basketball, WC Tennis, Nordic Skiing/Biathlon, Snow Shoeing, Fly--fishing, Cycling, Archery, Disc Golf	$51,009.00	VA Maine, University of New Hampshire, New England Nordic Ski Assoc., MedStar NRP
MI	Michigan Sports Unlimited PO Box 200, Essexville, MI 48732	Track & Field, Archery, Air Rifle, Powerlifting, Swimming, Handcycling	$20,000.00	Saginaw VA, Wheelchair & Ambulatory Sports USA, Michigan PVA
NC	Bridge II Sports 4122 Bennett Memorial Road, Suite 105 Durham NC 27705-	Air---rifle and Archery, Kayaking, Sitting VB/Boccia, Shot Put, Rowing,	$151,000.00	Durham VA, Fayetteville VA, Duke University, University of NC at Chapel Hill, Triangle Volleyball Club, National Rifle

		REGIONAL PARTNERS		
STATE	ORGANIZATION	ADAPTIVE SPORTS	AMOUNT	PARTNERS
	1209	Powerlifting, Table Tennis, Cycling		Assoc., US Olympic Committee
NH	University of New Hampshire Sponsored Programs Administration 51 College Road Durham, NH 03824--3585	Aquatics, Sled hockey, Cycling, Fishing, Alpine, Nordic, snowshoe, waterskiing, kayaking, Archery and Boccia.	$298,206.00	VAMCs in Central Western Massachusetts, Manchester, Togus White River Junction, Gaylord Sports Association, Ability Plus, The Granite YMCA
PA	Two Top Mountain Adaptive Sports Fnd. 10914 Clay Lick Road Mercersburg, PA 17236	Alpine Skiing, Snowboarding, Waterskiing, Kayaking, Cycling	$89,280.00	Disabled Sport USA, Adaptive Adventures, Mission Continues, Hampton Road USO, Walter Reed NMMC, Ft. Belvoir
TX	Heroes on the Water 101-C N. Greenville Ave. #55, Allen, TX 75002	Kayaking, Fishing	$65,000.00	Lake City VA, R4 Alliance
TX	LS Classic Foundation 1215 Red River, 1st Floor Austin, TX 78701	Multi-Sport events throughout Texas	$120,000.00	San Antonio VA, Houston VA, Dallas VA, Waco VA, Temple VA, Lone Star PVA, Travis County Veterans Services
TX	San Antonio Sports Foundation P.O. Box 830386, San Antonio, TX 78283-0386	Valor Games Southeast, Archery, Air Guns, Kayaking, Powerlifting	$161,000.00	VAMCs in Dallas, Houston and San Antonio, Brooke Army Medical Center, USA Shooting, USA Archery, USA Powerlifting, Operation Comfort
TX	Sport, Outdoor and Recreation (SOAR) 5223 David Edwards Dr., San Antonio, TX 78233	Soccer, WC Football, WC Softball, Boccia, Goalball, WC Basketball	$64,996.00	San Antonio VA, South Texas PVA, Brooke Army Medical Center, Wounded Warrior Project, Operation Comfort
UT	National Ability Center 1000 Ability Way, P.O. Box 682799, Park City, UT 84060	Skiing/Snowboarding, Equestrian Activities, Cycling, Archery, Sled Hockey, Water Sports	$104,588.00	Boise VA, Salt Lake City VA, San Diego Naval Medical Center, University of Utah
VA	American Canoe Association 503 Sophia St. Suite 100 Fredericksburg, VA 22401	Flatwater Kayaking, Whitewater Kayaking, Flatwater Canoeing	$149,133.85	USA Canoe/Kayak, Town of Quantico Va.
VA	Crossroads Adaptive Athletic Alliance 1302 Earnestins St., McLean,	Crossfit, Functional Fitness	$118,920.00	Team RWB, CrossFit Rubicon, Reebok CrossFit Bare Cove, CrossFit Redefined, CrossFit

(Continued)

		REGIONAL PARTNERS		
STATE	ORGANIZATION	ADAPTIVE SPORTS	AMOUNT	PARTNERS
	VA 22101			VA Beach, CrossFit Exchange, Blue Titan Fitness, CrossFit Pisgah, CrossFit Pittsburgh
WA	VetBikes.org 2501 53rd Way SE, Olympia, WA 98501	Cycling	$73,980.00	Seattle VA., Palo Alto VA, Joint Base Lewis-McChord, Fort Carson, Washington State Veterans Affairs, Catholic Community Services at Michael's Place, Compass Housing Authority
WI	Central Cross Country Ski Association P.O. Box 930442, Verona, WI 53593	Nordic Skiing, Biathlon	$65,450.00	VAMCs in Chicago, Milwaukee, Minneapolis, Rehabilitation Institute of Chicago, Blackhawk Ski Club, U.S. Paralympics
	TOTAL		$2,578,179.27	
		COMMUNITY---BASED PROGRAMS		
STATE	ORGANIZATION	ADAPTIVE SPORTS	AMOUNT	PARTNERS
AL	Lakeshore Foundation 4000 Ridgeway Dr. Birmingham, AL 35209---5563	Archery, Biathlon, Boccia, Cycling, Paratriathlon, Swimming, W/C Rugby, W/C Basketball, Hockey, Powerlifting	$31,757.89	Birmingham VA
CA	Incight 45480 Portola Ave., Palm Desert, CA 92260	Ropes Course, Kayaking, Throwing (Discus, Shot Put, Javelin), WC Tennis or Basketball, Cycling	$28,095.00	PVA California, Desert Recreation District
CA	Riekes Center for Human Enhancement 3455 Edison Way Menlo Park CA 94025-1813	Powerlifting, Archery, Tai Chi, Wheelchair Rugby, Track & Field, Shooting, Biathlon, Sitting Volleyball	$52,570.00	VA Palo Alto, US Paralympics, Valor Games, Northern CA Paralympic Regional Sport Program
CO	Adaptive Sports Center of Crested Butte P.O. Box 1639, Crested Butte, CO 81224	Skiing/Snowboarding, Cycling, Paddling, Climbing, Horseback Riding	$57,194.00	Denver VA, Fort Carson, Team R4V Inc., Racing for Veterans
CO	City of Fort Collins P.O. Box 580, 215 N. Mason- 3rd Floor Fort Collins, CO 80522---0580	Swimming, Cycling, Boccia	$15,000.00	Cheyenne VA, Colorado State University Center for Community Partnership

		COMMUNITY---BASED PROGRAMS		
STATE	ORGANIZATION	ADAPTIVE SPORTS	AMOUNT	PARTNERS
CO	Telluride Adaptive Sports Program P.O. Box 2254, Telluride, CO 81435	Skiing, Snowboarding, Rock/Ice Climbing, Cycling, Kayaking, Rafting, Canoeing, Fly Fishing, Golf	$58,000.00	Grand Junction VA, Fort Carson
FL	Veterans Ocean Adventures 20810 SW 86th Ave, Cutler Bay, FL 33189	Adaptive SCUBA Diving	$45,460.00	Miami VA, US Southern Command, Veterans Adaptive Sports, University of Miami, Florida DAV
HI	Ba Mamala Hoe Canoe Club 41-052 Hihimanu St., Waimanalo, HI 96795	Outrigger Paddling	$59,844.75	Wounded Warrior Project, Tripler Army Medical Center
IL	Revelation Golf P.O. Box 91831, Elk Grove, IL 60009	Golf	$60,000.00	Lovell Federal Healthcare Center, North Chicago VA
IN	Turnstone Center 3320 North Clinton St., Fort Wayne, IN 46805	Goalball, Basketball, Curling, Cycling, Archery	$47,039.00	US Assoc. of Blind Athletes, Fort Wayne Base Community Council, Trine Univ., Indiana Univ.--- Purdue Univ. Fort Wayne Military Student Services, Ivy Tech Comm. College, SRT Prosthetics and Orthotics, Brightpoint, Fort Wayne Curling Club
MA	All Out Adventures 214 State St., Northampton, MA 01060	Cycling	$20,204.00	VA Central Western Massachusetts, Massachusetts Universal Access Program, Look Park
MA	Holyoke Rows, Inc. PO Box 4936, Holyoke, MA 01041---4936	Rowing, kayaking	$18,000.00	Leeds VA, Veterans Kayak and Rowing, Universal Access, Soldier On
MO	Disabled Athlete Sports Assn. 1236 Jungerman Rd Suite A St. Peters, MO 63376--- 6962	Sled Hockey, Alpine Snow Ski, Archery, Track & Field, Handcycle, Triathlon, Road Racing, FUNctional fitness	$48,815.00	St Louis VA, Fort Leonard Wood, Southwest Wheelchair Athletic Association, Wheelchair & Ambulatory Sports USA
NV	City of Reno 1 East 1st St., Reno, NV 89501	General Fitness, Cycling, Powerlifting	$20,000.00	Reno VA, R4 Alliance, Ride 2 Recovery, Westcare
NY	Buffalo Warriors Hockey, Inc. 2607 Niagara St.,	Sled Hockey	$22,550.00	Buffalo VA, USA Hockey

(Continued)

		COMMUNITY---BASED PROGRAMS		
STATE	ORGANIZATION	ADAPTIVE SPORTS	AMOUNT	PARTNERS
	Buffalo, NY 14207---1029			
NY	Capital Region Nordic Alliance Inc. 28 Eileen St., Albany, NY 12203	XC Skiing, Biathlon, Orienteering, Snowshoeing, Trailrunning	$48,784.00	Albany VA, Albany Housing Coalition, Adaptive Sports Foundation
NY	Fencers Club 229 W. 28th Street, 2nd Fl., New York, NY 10001	Fencing	$29,189.00	VISN 3
NY	Hudson River Community Sailing PO Box 20677, New York, NY 10002	Sailing	$30,000.00	VA New York Harbor
NY	Move Along Inc. P.O. Box 5220, Oswego, NY 13126	W/C Basketball, Sled Hockey, Handcycling, Kayaking	$26,205.00	Syracuse VA, Clear Path for Veterans
OH	City of Columbus Recreation and Parks 1111 E. Broad St., Columbus, OH 43205	Bowling, Yoga, Fitness Training, Sled Hockey, Boccia, Swimming	$61,564.50	Chillicothe VA, Columbus VA, DAV Chapter 3, Greater Columbus Rowing Association, Ohio Warrior Hockey Program, Yoga on High
PA	Slippery Rock University of Pennsylvania 1 Morrow Way Slippery Rock, PA 16057---1326	Equine Therapy	$52,092.00	Butler VA, Pittsburgh VA, Cleveland VA, PVA, Three Rivers Adapted Sports, Student Vet. of America
SC	Greenville Health System 701 Grove Road, Greenville, SC 29605	Sled Hockey, Golf, Skiing, Cycling, Handcycling, Water Skiing, Sailing.	$81,201.00	Upstate Warrior Solution, Honoring Their Service
TN	Tennessee Association for Blind Athletes P.O. Box 160185, Nashville, TN 37216	Goalball, Bowling, Tandem---cycling, Kickball, Fitness/Nutrition, Archery, Basketball, Golf, Baseball, Disc Golf	$47,164.00	Memphis VA, Blinded Veterans of America
TX	University of Texas at Arlington 701 S. Nedderman Dr., Box 19145 Arlington, TX 76019---0145	W/C Basketball, W/C Tennis, Fitness Training, Hand Cycling, Table Tennis,	$70,350.00	VA North Texas Health System

		COMMUNITY---BASED PROGRAMS		
STATE	ORGANIZATION	ADAPTIVE SPORTS	AMOUNT	PARTNERS
		Track and Field, Weightlifting		
UT	Fuel Trainer 2468 Beagle Drive, Sandy, UT 84092	Cycling, Sports Nutrition	$50,816.92	
UT	University of Utah 75 South 2000 East Salt Lake City, Utah 84112-8930	Biathlon, Cross Country Skiing, Handcycling, Kayaking, Swimming, WC Tennis, Fitness	$30,000.00	VA Salt Lake City
VT	Vermont Adaptive Ski & Sports P.O. Box 139 Killington, VT 05751	Skiing & Biathlon, Snowshoeing, Canoe, Kayak, Camping/backcoun try, Handcycling, Sailing	$43,163.00	VT Dept. of Labor, United Spinal Assoc., Home Base Program, Vermont Veterans Outreach Program, 10th Mountain Div. Foundation
WA	Metropolitan Park District of Tacoma 4702 S 19th St., Tacoma, WA 98405- --1175	W/C Basketball, Goalball, Archery, Swimming, Rugby, Kayaking, Cycling	$65,000.00	Joint Base Lewis-McChord, American Lake VA, Seattle VA, PVA Washington, Outdoors for All, Northwest Assoc. for Blind Athletes
WI	AFAR Inc. 10700 W. Research Dr., Suite 100 Milwaukee, WI 53226	Wheelchair Lacrosse	$40,000.00	Milwaukee VA, PVA Wisconsin, Marquette University, University of Wisconsin
	TOTAL		$1,260,059.06 $7,999,946.28	

INDEX

G

H

I

J

K

L

M

N

O

P

Q

R

S

T

U

V

W